FROM READER TO WRITER

WITHDRAWN

GARY LIBRARY
VERMONT COLLEGE
COLLEGE STREET
MONTPELIER, VT 05602

WITHDRAWN

Please remember that this is a library book,
and that it belongs only temporarily to each
person who uses it. Be considerate. Do
not write in this, or any, library book.

Please remember that this is a library book,
and that it belongs only temporarily to each

FROM READER TO WRITER
TEACHING WRITING THROUGH CLASSIC CHILDREN'S BOOKS

SARAH ELLIS

A GROUNDWOOD BOOK
DOUGLAS & McINTYRE
VANCOUVER TORONTO BUFFALO

372.623044
E471f
2001

Excerpt from *O Beloved Kids, Letters from Rudyard Kipling to His Son* reprinted by permission of A.P. Watt Ltd. on behalf of The National Trust for Places of Historic Interest or Natural Beauty. Excerpts from *Selected Letters* and *Journals* of Louisa May Alcott reprinted by permission of Joel Myerson, University of South Carolina. Excerpt from *The Tale of Peter Rabbit* by Beatrix Potter copyright © Frederick Warne & Co., 1902. Reproduced by kind permission of Frederick Warne & Co. Excerpts from *Letters to Children from Beatrix Potter* copyright © Frederick Warne & Co., 1992. Reproduced by kind permission of Frederick Warne & Co. Excerpts from *A Letter to a Friend*, *Swallows and Amazons* and *Signalling from Mars: The Letters of Arthur Ransome* reprinted by permission of Jonathan Cape Excerpts from *The Letters of Lewis Carroll* reprinted by permission of A. P. Watt Ltd. on behalf of The Trustees of the C.L. Dodgson Estate and Morton Cohen. Excerpts from *The Selected Journals of L.M. Montgomery, Volumes I and II* © 1985, 1987 University of Guelph, ed. by Mary Rubio and Elizabeth Waterston, and published by Oxford University Press Canada, are reproduced with the permission of Mary Rubio, Elizabeth Waterston and the University of Guelph, courtesy of the L.M. Montgomery Collection Archival and Special Collections, University of Guelph Library. Excerpts from *My Dear Mr. M.* and *The Green Gables Letters* are printed with the permission of Ruth Macdonald. *My Dear Mr. M.: Letters to George MacMillan from L.M. Montgomery* is published by Oxford University Press Canada 1992. *The Green Gables Letters* is published by Borealis Press 1982. *L. M. Montgomery* is a trademark of the Heirs of L. M. Montgomery Inc.

Copyright © 2000 by Sarah Ellis
First paperback edition 2001

All rights reserved. No part of this book may be reproduced, stored in a retrieval system or transmitted in any form or by any means, without the prior written permission of the publisher or, in the case of photocopying or other reprographic copying, a licence from CANCOPY (Canadian Reprography Collective), Toronto, Ontario.

We acknowledge the financial support of the Canada Council for the Arts, the Ontario Arts Council and the Government of Canada through the Book Publishing Industry Development Program for our publishing activities.

ONTARIO ARTS COUNCIL
CONSEIL DES ARTS DE L'ONTARIO

Groundwood Books / Douglas & McIntyre
720 Bathurst Street, Suite 500, Toronto, Ontario M5S 2R4

Distributed in the USA by Publishers Group West,
1700 Fourth Street, Berkeley, CA 94710

National Library of Canada Cataloguing in Publication Data
Ellis, Sarah
From reader to writer : teaching writing through classic children's books
A Groundwood book.
Includes index.
ISBN 0-88899-372-2 (bound) ISBN 0-88899-440-0 (pbk.)
1. English language - Composition and exercises - Study and teaching (Elementary).
2. Children's literature - Study and teaching (Elementary). I. Title.
LB1576.E445 2001   372.62'3044   C00-930399-5

Printed and bound in Canada

CONTENTS

Introduction: On Learning to Write / 9

How to Use This Book / 11

Islands of the Mind: Robert Louis Stevenson / 14

Kin Stories: Jean Little / 25

Fairies in Our Midst: P.L. Travers / 33

Clip and Write: Monica Hughes / 43

Summers on the Lake: Arthur Ransome / 53

Bird-Man of the Arctic and Other Imaginary Beings:
    Michael Kusugak / 62

E.S.L. — Elvish as a Second Language: J.R.R. Tolkien / 68

Write While You Sleep: Susan Cooper / 78

Yours Affectionately: Beatrix Potter / 87

Digging Up Stories: Paul Yee / 102

A Bag of Tricks: Lewis Carroll / 108

Book Breeding: Kit Pearson / 124

Piano Four Hands: C.S. Lewis / 132

A Picture and a Thousand Words: Virginia Hamilton /140

A Tale of Two Journals: Louisa May Alcott
    and L. M. Montgomery / 146

On the Outside Looking In: Katherine Paterson / 159

Index / 169

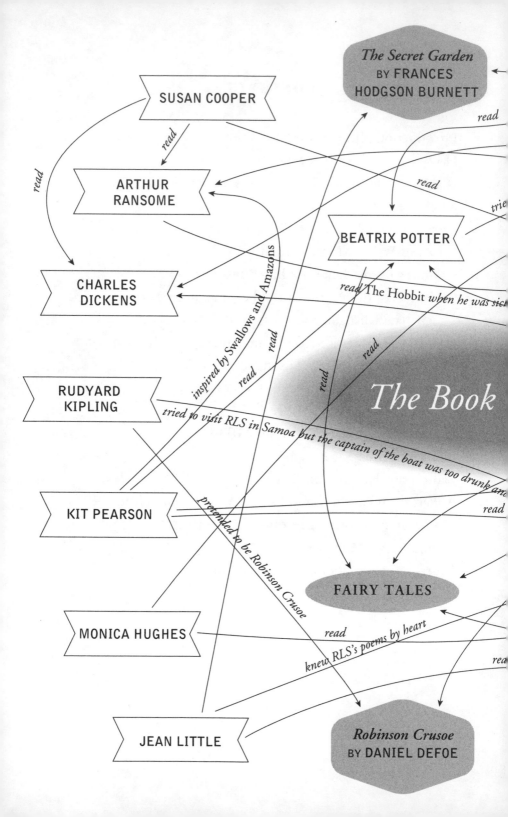

The Secret Garden BY FRANCES HODGSON BURNETT

SUSAN COOPER

read

ARTHUR RANSOME

read

read

CHARLES DICKENS

BEATRIX POTTER

read

trie

read The Hobbit when he was sick

inspired by Swallows and Amazons

read

read

read

read

RUDYARD KIPLING

The Book

tried to visit RLS in Samoa but the captain of the boat was too drunk and

read

KIT PEARSON

pretended to be Robinson Crusoe

FAIRY TALES

MONICA HUGHES

read

knew RLS's poems by heart

rea

JEAN LITTLE

Robinson Crusoe BY DANIEL DEFOE

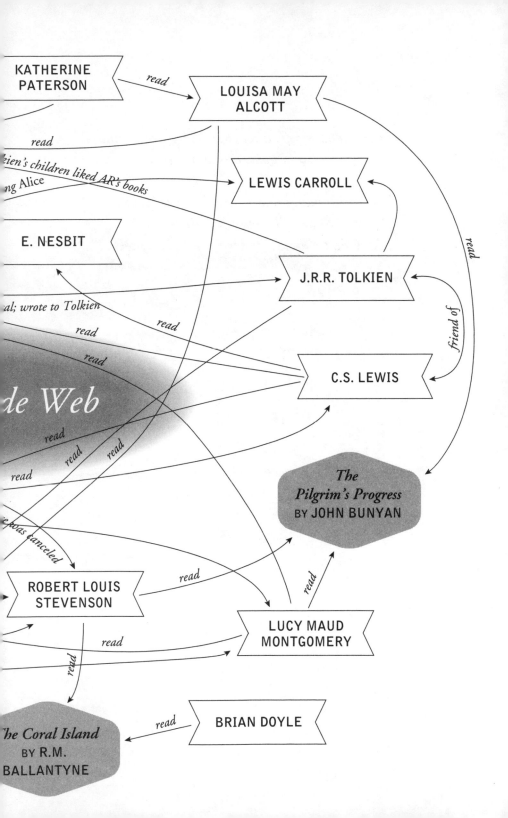

KATHERINE PATERSON

read → LOUISA MAY ALCOTT

read

...ien's children liked AR's books

...ng Alice → LEWIS CARROLL

E. NESBIT

J.R.R. TOLKIEN

al; wrote to Tolkien

read

read

de Web

read

C.S. LEWIS

friend of

read

read

read

read

read

The *Pilgrim's Progress* BY JOHN BUNYAN

...e was fancied

ROBERT LOUIS STEVENSON

read →

read

LUCY MAUD MONTGOMERY

read

read

read

he Coral Island BY R.M. BALLANTYNE

read ← BRIAN DOYLE

For Sheila Egoff, a teacher of rigorous mind and generous spirit.

With many thanks to Russ McMath and Sheilagh Martin—
"And gladly wolde he lerne and gladly teche."

INTRODUCTION:
ON LEARNING TO WRITE

Can creative writing be taught? Writers themselves, a quirky and intractable bunch, offer no united front on this issue. Some, in the independent "I did it my way" school, answer with an adamant No. Learning to write is like learning to roller-blade, they assert. Forget the theory. Just strap on your skates and head to the nearest hill. These writers are characterized by determination and the willingness to take risks. They will proudly tell you that they failed high-school English.

In the opposing camp are writers who regard their discipline as a subject that can be learned. For them, learning to write is like learning to do your own plumbing. You need skills and tools, and the best way to learn is to apprentice yourself to a plumber. Writers in this group are characterized by hard work. They say things like "Writing is easy. You just sit in front of a piece of paper until beads of blood appear on your forehead."

A subgroup in favor of the teaching of writing are the group learners. These are folks who write in tandem or who belong to manuscript reading groups and writers' Listservs. They are characterized by a delight in community and a deep desire to communicate. You can identify them by their tendency to say, "I don't know where I would be without my writing group."

So who is right? The proof is obviously in the pudding—the rich, delectable word-pudding of literature. Put in your thumb and pull out a plum and it could be an exemplar of any of the above groups or a myriad others. In writing, unlike in pantyhose, one size does not fit all.

Young writers are as varied a group as old ones. In this book my aim is to provide writing ideas and inspiration for all kinds of learners—the roller-bladers who need solitude and freedom, the plumbers who need structure, and the joiners who need company. My inspiration, while researching this book, was a group of classic children's writers that I have come to know through their essays, journals, letters, memoirs and autobiographies. They are excellent company, and they can provide for children a pageant of variety—variety of motivation, method and personality.

Although my gang of fellow scribblers revealed itself to be as motley a crew as can be imagined, I did find several areas of common ground. These commonalities have informed my approach in two ways. The first is that all the writers were readers. Writing and reading are inextricably linked. Therefore, I have included in this celebration of writing both information on what the writers read, and book lists with suggestions for further reading, including reading aloud.

The second truth that linked my company of writers is that writing involves pleasure. Above all, the ideas in this book are meant to provide young writers with a taste of the pleasures of writing, for the freedom, exhilaration and deep satisfaction of finding just the right words.

HOW TO USE THIS BOOK

This book is designed to inspire reading, writing, and/or talking. The ideas are adaptable to long- and short-term projects and to both individuals and groups of various sizes. Along the way I have provided guidelines as to age suitability and classroom or workshop application.

Each chapter hinges on an anecdote from the life of a well-known children's writer, mostly focusing on an incident from his or her childhood. It is very satisfying for children to discover that their contemporaries in the past were bored, lonely, grouchy, bad, bullied, absent-minded or weird. These anecdotes also contain revealing glimpses of life in the olden days—children who hardly ever saw their parents, a young boy sent to boarding school, a little girl in an experimental commune, growing up in a family of eleven siblings. The stories can be used as springboards to discussions of history. Students might notice, for example, how much unsupervised, unstructured time children had in the past, and compare this to the pace of their own lives.

The anecdotes can also be used as an introduction to an author, a kind of mini author visit (which conveniently can include the dead as well as the living!), a short teaser for a book talk on *Mary Poppins* or *M.C. Higgins the*

Great or *The Lion, the Witch and the Wardrobe.*

In terms of writing, the stories demonstrate to children that the ordinary experiences of their lives can be the material for fiction. J.R.R. Tolkien's amazing fantasy world began with the childhood game of making up words. Katherine Paterson felt excluded as a child, and out of these feelings came a bookshelf of deeply moving books. Lewis Carroll liked to do magic tricks when he was a kid, and when he grew up, he kept doing them, with words. It is one thing to tell a young writer, "Write about what you know." It is another to show them that that is exactly what these writers did.

Each anecdote is followed by a section focusing on a specific book. This section includes a read-aloud suggestion. These excerpts are designed to stand on their own without too much background and to give the listener a genuine sense of the *flavor* of the book. So much of feeling comfortable with a book is having a sense of how it sounds in your head before you start. This comfort comes easily with a contemporary novel but can be a bit more challenging with a fantasy, history or book from the past.

For older students the read-alouds also have a writing application as a springboard for noticing technique. How does Virginia Hamilton maintain tension? What does Monica Hughes do with point of view?

The emphasis then shifts more directly to writing, with a specific writing project. Some can be tackled in a once-over-lightly one-hour session and are thus suited to a one-time workshop. Others need research and collaboration or can only be done over time, thus making them more appropriate for an on-going group. I've written these sections addressing the students directly. You can therefore use them as a script. This style of address also underscores my conviction that you should do the exercises yourself to get a sense of their potential and difficulties. (And also because you will probably enjoy them and may well [re]discover your own pleasure in writing.)

To bring us back to the symbiotic relationship between writing and reading I have also included information, where possible, on what the writers read as children. The purpose here is to show that writing grows from reading and that writers are not alone. For a visual demonstration of this connection, please see the writing/reading web on pages 6 and 7. This web looks like a gathering of the famous, but as soon as a child has read one of the books mentioned on it, he or she joins its network.

The final section is an annotated book list. It can be used as a resource for titles to read aloud to classes, to provide reading guidance to individual readers, to extend your own knowledge of children's literature or to build a classroom library. If the chapter is being used in an extended unit, students could each choose a different book from the list and then describe how the author uses letters or an object from the past or imaginary beings or human emotion. (This kind of focus often helps with the "book report blues.") The book lists also serve to extend the scope of possible reading from picture books to adult books, and to prove that not all splendid children's books are "classics."

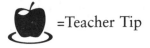 =Teacher Tip

Islands of the Mind:
Robert Louis Stevenson

Robert Louis Stevenson, known as Louis, was a very peculiar little boy. He was so skinny that people said it looked as if his bones would poke through his clothes. The damp climate of his Scottish home made his weak lungs worse, and he was sick more often than he was well. An only child, he never attended school regularly and he had few friends. If you had seen him sitting in an Edinburgh park in 1856, pale, weak and overprotected by his stern Calvinistic nanny, you might have felt sorry for him.

Yet, like many solitary Victorian children, Louis had a rich imaginative life. He could make a whole world out of anything—a toy theater, lead soldiers, Bible stories, tales his nanny told him, his own terrifying nightmares. When he passed by a graveyard, he would put his ear to the stone wall and pretend to hear the voices of the dead.

Some of Louis's happiest times were spent in the company of his cousins. Cousin Bob in particular was a congenial and sympathetic playmate. Together they invented imaginary kingdoms. Bob's was called Nosingtonia and Louis invented a world called Encyclopedia. The raw material for these inventions was everywhere, including breakfast.

In an essay called "Child's Play," the grown Robert Louis Stevenson remembers his kingdom of porridge:

When my cousin and I took our porridge of a morning, we had a device to enliven the course of a meal. He ate his with sugar, and explained it to be a country continually buried under snow. I took mine with milk, and explained it to be a country suffering gradual inundation. You can imagine us exchanging bulletins; how here was an island still unsubmerged, here a valley not yet covered with snow; what inventions were made; how his population lived in cabins on perches and travelled on stilts, and how mine was always in boats; how the interest grew furious, as the last corner of safe ground was cut off on all sides and grew smaller every moment.

Years later, Louis, a grown man with a wife and career and stepchildren, was vacationing in a small cottage. The weather was bad and things were getting a bit tense in the enclosed space. To entertain his stepson Lloyd, Stevenson produced some watercolor paints and suggested that the boy draw a map of an island. To keep Lloyd company, Stevenson joined in with his own map.

What he produced kindled his imagination:

It was elaborately and (I thought) beautifully coloured; the shape of it took my fancy beyond expression; it contained harbours that pleased me like sonnets and with the unconsciousness of the predestined I ticketed my performance Treasure Island. . . . as I pored upon my map of Treasure Island the future characters of the book began to appear there visibly among imaginary woods; and their brown faces and bright weapons peeped out upon me from

unexpected quarters, as they passed to and fro, fight-
ing and hunting treasure, on these few square inches
of a flat projection. The next thing I knew, I had
some paper before me and was writing out a list of
chapters.

So began a furious fifteen-day writing frenzy in which
Louis wrote the first fifteen chapters of *Treasure Island.*
Writer Pierre Berton calls it "the best boy's book ever
written." This pirate adventure story has been enjoyed by
readers for more than one hundred years.

What Did Robert Louis Stevenson Read?
Louis's interest in islands was certainly inspired in part by
his reading. His favorite book when he was a boy was *The
Coral Island,* a castaway story by fellow Scot R.M.
Ballantyne. *The Coral Island* is a "Robinsonnade," a type
of desert island story inspired originally by *Robinson
Crusoe* and a highly popular genre in the nineteenth century. (Writer Brian Doyle was also influenced by *The
Coral Island,* not so much for its adventurous plot as for
its archaic language. He remembers the delight of encountering the word "cogitations" on its pages.) Louis also
read *The Arabian Nights*, which inspired him to write his
own collection of tales called *The New Arabian Nights.*
Other early attempts at writing were inspired by the Bible.
   Louis's first work, written when he was six and illustrated by himself, was "A History of Moses." In common
with many middle-class Victorian children, Louis also
read, or had read to him, John Bunyan's seventeenth-cen-
tury allegory *The Pilgrim's Progress*. Another favorite
read-aloud was Shakespeare. Louis's mother read
Macbeth to him when he was very young.
   Louis's grown-up taste for blood and thunder might

have had something to do with the ghosts and treachery and witches of *Macbeth*, but it was also probably inspired by his childhood taste for junk. On Saturdays he and his nanny would stand at the windows of news agents to read stories in the scandal papers—stories of murders, haunted houses and bodies discovered in pits.

For more descriptions of influential books in the lives of famous people see *Everybody's Favourites: Canadians Talk About Books That Changed Their Lives* by Arlene Perly Rae. Bring one of your own childhood favorites to class. Canvas your colleagues and display all their favorite books from childhood. Encourage children to ask their parents and other adult friends for this information.

Treasure Island: A Sneak Preview and Read-Aloud Suggestion

Jim, who tells us the story of Treasure Island, begins his seafaring adventures because he comes into possession of an island treasure map. How does he get this map? It all involves a set of visitors to the isolated coastal inn that his parents own—a set of very sinister visitors. Dirty, ugly, violent, cutlass-wielding ex-shipmates, this gang is seriously scary. In the opening chapters Robert Louis Stevenson introduces us to these villains and then does away with two of them. One is terrified into a fatal fit and another is trampled to death by charging horses. Jim ends up with the map, and there is much more villainy to come.

On board the treasure-seeking ship *Hispaniola* are Jim, Captain Smollet, a couple of good guys—Dr. Livesay and Squire Trelawney—various crew members and, most important, the ship's cook, the one-legged Long John Silver, who is not what he seems. After Jim overhears Silver planning a mutiny with the crew, things get very complicated and interesting. A group of men, greedy for gold, willing to kill for it, isolated on a small ship and then on a small island. Who is to be trusted? Who has the power? Who's going to stab you in the back, and when? Jim, who does a lot of sneaking and eavesdropping (and a bit of shooting of his own), knows more than anyone else. In two feats of bravery and trickiness he saves the day and earns his part of the treasure.

Greed, violence, suspense and a one-legged cutthroat that you end up half liking. An old pirate who sings, "Yo ho ho and a bottle full of rum," and a parrot who screams, "Pieces of eight, pieces of eight." The first person to read *Treasure Island* was Stevenson's thirteen-year-old stepson. He thought it was a great read. He was right.

Much of the appeal of *Treasure Island* lies in the setting. A tropical island—picture the travel brochure. Crashing surf, golden sunshine, delicious fruit hanging from the trees, the smell of flowers in the air. Robert Louis Stevenson plays with this expectation in a pair of scenes in Chapter 14. The chapter opens with Jim wandering around the island on his own. The sun is shining on the hills, trees are in blossom, a snake suns itself on a rock and Jim is filled with "the joy of exploration." We are lulled into lazy contentment along with our hero. Abruptly the mood changes as Jim hears the approaching voices of Long John Silver and his mates. Jim crawls into the underbrush to spy on the desperadoes. From his hiding place he listens in as one of the men, Tom, attempts to defy Silver's authority. Jim then witnesses the murder of Tom by Silver.

The four paragraphs in which this murder are described are an excellent example of effective horror writing. Stevenson uses sensual details, particularly that of sound, the panting of Silver as he buries his knife in Tom.

We also see in this scene the power of describing not the horror but the effect of the horror. At one point in the action Stevenson pulls back and describes the effect of the events on Jim, who becomes dizzy and faint. At the end of this scene Jim suddenly realizes that if he were discovered, he could well be the next murder victim.

A tropical island—paradise or prison? *Treasure Island* is both.

For the younger writer *Treasure Island* provides an excellent example of suspense and adventure writing. For the slightly older reader it also presents an interesting character study in Long John Silver, the wicked but attractive villain. A look at various illustrated editions reveals the ambiguity of his character. Ralph Steadman makes him look like a homicidal maniac. In Robert Ingpen's portrait he is worn and introspective. C.B. Falls pictures him as a dandy. In the Walt Disney movie he is a cartoon-like buffoon. Illustrator N.C. Wyeth keeps Silver's face in shadow and lets us imagine.

Ask students to hunt up several different editions of *Treasure Island* and compare the illustrations. Discuss which one makes you want to read the book. What is the best way to portray a menacing character? If you were the artist, what medium or style would you choose?

Robert Louis Stevenson's style is more ornate than the plainer, more journalistic style that most children are used to, and this action-packed adventure will be best enjoyed by students in grade six and older.

Island Writing Project:
A Classroom Script

Islands provide good springboards to story because they are contained and isolated. The containment gives you a shape or structure. The isolation gives you the freedom to imagine. There is also something universal in our fascination with islands. In 1913, J.M. Barrie of *Peter Pan* fame wrote an introduction to *Coral Island* that began with the sentence, "To be born is to be wrecked on an island."

See what it was like to be Robert Louis Stevenson. Take a blank piece of paper and draw the shape of an island. Fiddle with your island until the shape pleases you.

What is the coastline like? Does it have coves, bays, inlets, gulfs, harbors? What about firths, estuaries, bights? For inspiration browse through an atlas.

Now you have the outline of a whole world and a lot of questions.

Some things to think about:

• Is this island in an ocean? In a lake, a lagoon? How about an island in a frozen sea or an island that rises mysteriously out of an impassable desert? Is it still an island if it's not surrounded by water? You get to choose.

• Ups and downs. Are there hills, valleys, plateaus, mesas, mountains? Are the mountains volcanic? Is the terrain steep or gentle? Are there beaches, cliffs? Draw in these features or color the island like a topographical map. Doodling with your island, sketching in a range of pointed mountains or cross-hatching a plain can help focus your mind and put you in an imaginative, storytelling mood.

• Water. Are there rivers? Are they wide and lazy or dangerous with white water and rapids? What about lakes, swamps or marshes? Maybe there is quicksand.

• Name the features of your island. This is a good chance

to make up words. If you need a jump-start, browse through the index of an atlas: Qatar, Qin Ling Shan, Quaco Head, Quantz Lake, Quatre Bras, Queen Bess Mountain. If somebody is making your life miserable, you can name a mosquito-ridden, pestilent bog after them.

• Weather and climate. Cold or hot? Dry or wet? Windy or still? Moderate or extreme? How many seasons? Is there rain? Snow, hail, fog? Where do the winds come from? Are there droughts, storms, hurricanes, tornadoes, thunderstorms?

• Plants and animals. Insects, fish and reptiles. How about field guides to your island? Use real plants and animals or invent your own. What about micro-organisms? What is edible?

At some point your island will start to seem real to you. That's a good time to visit it. Swim to its shores or float in on a log. Pull your canoe (raft, rubber dinghy, rowboat) onto the shore; moor your sailboat (submarine, hydroplane, yacht) or find a landing place for your helicopter (dirigible, fighter-bomber, biplane). Get out and take a walk.

What does it smell like? What do you hear? What does the air feel like? What are the colors of your island? Do you feel safe here? What's that movement just around the curve in the path?

Walk around your island. At this point you will probably find a story.

What kind of a story will your island reveal? It might be action-packed like *Treasure Island*. It might be quiet or funny or just plain weird. Maybe you'll encounter some people. Maybe you'll turn into a different person yourself. You might write the whole thing down at once, or you might tuck parts of it away in your head or your journal for later.

Lawrence Durrell invented the word "islomania" to describe the pleasure of knowing that you are in a place that is entirely surrounded by water. Join the islomaniacs and discover what stories lurk on your own personal island.

If you get stuck or tired, take a break. After all, you have just created a whole world.

Island-making can be a solitary activity. It can remain entirely private, or the island-maker can introduce the island to others by providing a guidebook or Home page for potential tourists. Island-making can also be a group project, either by creating the island through group discussion and input or by combining individual islands into an archipelago.

An Archipelago: Books Set on Islands

Brink, Carol Ryrie. *Baby Island*. Two sisters shipwrecked on an island with four babies. Now that's a babysitting challenge! This is a gentle, old-fashioned story with appeal to younger readers.

Cole, Brock. *The Goats*. Laura and Howie, marooned on a small island without their clothes, are the "goats"—victims of their fellow campers. How do they survive and keep their dignity? This novel raises many of the same ethical issues as *Lord of the Flies*.

Fry, Rosalie K. *The Secret of Roan Inish*. Fiona's baby brother was swept out to sea in his wooden cradle. There are rumors that he is still alive. What is the secret of the island of Roan Inish? Interesting to compare with the movie of the same name.

LeGuin, Ursula. *A Wizard of Earthsea*. Sparrowhawk is a young wizard in training on the island of Roke. He is talented but foolish and one day he unleashes a terrible power. Readers who take to this fantasy world will eat up the other three books in the series: *The Tombs of Atuan*, *The Farthest Shore* and *Tehanu*.

O'Dell, Scott. *Island of the Blue Dolphins*. Twelve-year-old Karana is abandoned on a Pacific island by her tribe. This historical novel is a stunning example of the use of a very limited cast of characters.

Macken, Walter. *Island of the Great Yellow Ox*. Three boys— one a toddler—encounter a couple of villains who will stop at nothing in their quest for the ancient treasure of the island. Bad guys and cliffhangers.

MacLachlan, Patricia. *Baby*. When the summer visitors leave Larkin's island, a baby is left behind. This brief understated book is vibrant with emotion.

Paterson, Katherine. *Jacob Have I Loved*. Twin sisters growing up on a small island. Caroline is beautiful and gifted, destined for great things. But what of Louisa? What is her destiny? A Newbery Award book.

Paulsen, Gary. *The Island*. Will's life is going down the toilet until he discovers the island, his place. Paulsen demonstates in this, as in his other books, a unique understanding of teenage boys.

Seabrooke, Brenda. *The Bridges of Summer*. Zarah finds out a lot about her heritage when she visits the island home of her grandmother, the daughter of slaves.

Steig, William. *Abel's Island*. Like any castaway Abel must find food and shelter. Unlike most castaways, Abel is a mouse. An excellent read-aloud for graduates of Steig's inimitable picture books.

Taylor, Theodore. *The Bomb*. Sorry Rinamu's Pacific island home is threatened. What can one sixteen-year-old boy do against the U.S. atomic weapons testing program?

Townsend, John Rowe. *The Islanders*. Two castaway teenagers are relieved that their desert island refuge is inhabited. Or are they? Suspense and fine writing.

Kin Stories:
Jean Little

It is Sunday afternoon. Jean's normally hectic house is quiet. Her father and brothers are outside playing. Her mother is curled up on a chair reading. Five-year-old Jean feels like a story. Not just any story but her own story. She picks up her baby book—an album of photos and notes—and creeps up onto her mother's lap. "What does this say?" Jean asks, pointing to the first page of the album. Her mother smiles. Jean has already heard this story many times before. But she needs to hear it again. Her mother begins, "It says you weighed seven pounds, six ounces when you were born . . ." Jean snuggles in for the rest of the familiar tale, how when she was born she couldn't see, but one day she reached for a spoon and her mother, realizing that Jean did have some vision, cried for joy.

We all need family stories—the familiar stories of who we are and where we came from. Jean was lucky. She grew up in a close family with many aunts, uncles, cousins, a grandmother—all willing to talk about their interesting lives. Jean tucked these stories away in her memory—a savings account of family history.

Fifty years later, Jean, by now the prolific and popular children's writer Jean Little, was still living with her mother and listening to her stories. In her many novels Jean had shaped these family stories into fiction. She had used the events of her own life—her early childhood in Taiwan, her move to Canada, a home that felt like a foreign place, the experience of feeling excluded, the experience of living with a disability, her place in her family—as the emotional heart of her novels. She had mastered the art of shaping and embroidering the past into a story. She decided to apply these skills to the events of her mother's life, to the stories she had enjoyed since childhood.

In *His Banner Over Me*, Jean Little tells of a bright, determined, capable young girl called Gorrie Gauld, who moves from her birthplace in Taiwan to the family home in Canada, who is separated from her missionary parents for five years, who enters medical school at age sixteen. In writing this novel Jean Little gathered together a wealth of family stories and then "'adjusted facts,' invented people, and joined bits and pieces sometimes to make a coherent story."

Did everything really happen just as Jean describes it? Probably not. Is it a true story? Absolutely.

Jean Little's own pair of autobiographies, *Little by Little* and *The Stars Come Out Within*, are among the best child-oriented autobiographies ever. They excerpt beautifully and provide many opportunities for discussions about families, disabilities and using stories to cope with life.

What Did Jean Little Read?

The Secret Garden, Anne of Green Gables, Rebecca of Sunnybrook Farm, Emily of New Moon, A Child's Garden of Verses, Little Lord Fauntleroy, Hans Brinker, the poems of Emily Dickinson, *Jane Eyre.*

As Jean writes in *Little by Little*, joining the public library was a magical experience.

From that day on, when I was chased home from school, I went straight to my library book. The moment I opened it, I stopped being "cross-eyed" Jean Little and instead became Rebecca of Sunnybrook Farm or Lord Fauntleroy. I wept over books, too, but those were healing tears. When I suffered with Emily Starr or Hans Brinker, I felt comforted. I and the book children I loved were all part of a great fellowship. I was not alone any longer.

His Banner Over Me:
A Sneak Preview and Read-Aloud
Suggestion

Disasters have a way of fixing memory at a certain spot. "Did that happen before or after the flood?" "Was that the Christmas Mom dropped the turkey?" Many people find that their first memory involves some sort of disaster, dislocation or trauma.

In Chapter 9 of *His Banner Over Me*, Jean Little tells the story of a cyclone that hits Regina. At this point in the story nine-year-old Gorrie's parents have just left for Taiwan, leaving Gorrie and her brother and sister in the care of an aunt. The sadness at the end of Chapter 8, filled with tearful goodbyes at the railway station, is dispelled by the action of the twister. The family crowds into the car and drives through a landscape of destruction to a neighboring town to check on Uncle Jim and Aunt Aggie. When they arrive it is to discover that these relatives have lost the roof of their house: "But the roof was gone and it looked as though someone had taken a huge spoon and stirred up everything in the house."

In this scene Jean Little combines a feeling of immediacy and freshness with the sense of an oft-told family story. Specific details—Aunt Aggie moaning as she sits in her destroyed home on the one intact chair, and hailstones as big as baseballs (a touch of the tall tale)—add up to a story that is familiar to us all, the story of a disaster that is at once sad and exciting, tragic and hilarious. In the midst of the storm the most unexpected people get the giggles.

The real-life Gorrie remembered this day her whole life. When she grew up she told the story to her daughter Jean. When Jean grew up she became a writer and told the story to us.

 Jean Little's books are very accessible to a wide age range and work well for grade three right through to junior high.

Jean Little mentions many books *within* her own books. Encourage students to see how many book titles they can find inside her novels. Create a poster of the findings. Find copies of the books and create a display.

Collecting and Writing Family Stories: A Classroom Script

Family stories are the icing on the family cake. They are fun, they connect you to your relatives, they give everybody a chance to show off. Family stories are especially valuable to the writer. Stories that are told over and over again and are passed from person to person get better with each telling. By the time you hear a family story it has already been polished and edited. And even though you didn't invent the story, you own it, just because you are part of your family.

You probably already know family stories. The time Uncle Mark crazy-glued his glasses to his nose. When

Judy mislaid the baby. The mysterious wedding guest. Caitlin's horrible job interview. The worst landlord in the world. How we finally found cousin Bruce's pet rat. The day Great-grandmother threw eggs at the horses. True love at the 7-11.

Sometimes people need encouragement to remember and tell family stories. A well-timed question at a family party, on a boring bus ride or while you're doing the dishes can often get things started.

Try these:

What is something I have in my life that you didn't have when you were a kid? What is something you had that I don't have?

Did you ever go to emergency? Have an operation, a cast?

What were you afraid of when you were little? What was the scariest thing that ever happened to you?

What were you not allowed to do when you were a kid? What was the worst thing you ever did? What did you do that your parents never knew about?

Did you move often? Houses, cities, countries? What was the best thing about the new place? What did you miss the most about the old?

Did you have a pet? Do you remember the day you got it? Who named it? Why?

Do you remember a time when a teacher was unfair? If you could meet one of your teachers now, who would you choose? Did you have a moment of triumph at school?

Was anyone in our family ever a victim of a crime?

What was the most amazing coincidence that you can remember?

What was your first job?

Did you ever have a weird neighbor?

Did you have a secret place as a child?

Were you ever in a flood? Ice storm? Tornado?

Ask your parents how they met.

Ask about the day you were born.

Ask how your name was chosen.

Family stories make a great addition to a writer's note-book. They don't need to be long or dramatic. Collect small incidents and details and you might share Jean Little's experience: "Always, for me, it is one small story that pulls me into writing a longer one."

A teacher's own experiences are always inspiring and fascinating to students. Answer the family story questions yourself and tell the students. (Censoring, of course, may be necessary!)

Our People: Family Stories

Cresswell, Helen. *Ordinary Jack*. The Bagthorpes are a talented family. They win prizes, medals, cups and certificates in swimming, karate, music, languages, electronics. Except for Jack, that is, eleven years old and ordinary. This is the story of Jack's hilarious quest for a place to shine.

Doyle, Brian. *Up to Low*. When young Tommy and his dad go off to the farm at Low, they enter a world of family. There are great-grandparents, grandparents and more aunts and uncles than you can keep track of. There is the neighbor family, Mean Hughie and all those kids. And don't forget the red-headed Hendricks. Tall tales rule.

Enright, Elizabeth. *The Saturdays*. One wet boring weekend the Melendy children form the Independent Saturday Afternoon Adventure Club. By pooling their four allowances, one of them gets to do something really great. And the others? They occupy the afternoon by doing something free, like inventing a cure for measles or burning the house down. (By mistake, of course.)

Estes, Eleanor. *The Moffats*. Jane hides in a box for a day to avoid a run-in with the chief of police. Rufus lends his precious tooth collection to improve the Halloween pumpkin. Joe teaches a dog to dance. Times are hard in the town of Cranbury and the Moffats are poor, but they never fail to have a good time.

Garnett, Eve. *The Family from One End Street*. There are a lot of Ruggles and their lives run from calamity to calamity. Lily Rose and the ironing disaster, Jim and the Gang of the Black Hand, John's ill-fated money-making scheme, baby William's quest for fame. It all adds up to one of the happiest families between two covers.

Gilbreth, Frank. *Cheaper by the Dozen*. The true (well, more or less) story of a family of twelve kids and their eccentric father. Mr. Gilbreth believes in efficiency in all things. The efficient bath (learn a foreign language while you get clean), the efficient dinner (learn times tables while eating), the efficient tonsil operation? Family life at its most uproarious.

Nesbit, E. *The Story of the Treasure Seekers*. When the Bastable family finances reach a crisis, the six Bastable children do the sensible thing and look for treasure. When traditional methods such as digging don't work out too well, they try solving crimes for the reward and selling poetry to newspapers. Then there's always finding a wealthy princess to marry or kidnapping somebody. The Bastables are not easily discouraged.

Streatfeild, Noel. *Ballet Shoes*. Great-uncle Matthew progresses from collecting fossils to collecting orphans. Pauline is rescued from an ocean liner that hits an iceberg. Petrova is found in a hospital. Posy is the gift of an impoverished young dancer. The living Fossils create an unusual family, especially when they take a vow to become famous.

Taylor, Sydney. *All-of-a-Kind Family*. Five sisters all dressed alike. They are poor in money but rich in stories, adventures and celebrations. Their father's junk store is an Aladdin's cave of delights. Purim, Passover and the Fourth of July are opportunities for feasting and visits. And then something happens that makes them not quite all of a kind.

Waterton, Betty. *Quincy Rumpel*. The Rumpels are a family with lots of ideas. The Rumpel Weed-Puller, the Rumpel Hygienic Toothbrush Holder, Rumpel Rebounders, mushroom growing, doorknob collecting. This spirit of do-it-yourself includes the kids. Ear-piercing, hair cuts, hair permanents? Why not just do it at home? There's never a dull moment when Quincy and her family are around.

Fairies in Our Midst:
P.L. Travers

"Once upon a time..." You know what's coming, right? It's going to be a fairy tale. There will be woodcutters, witches, queens, youngest sons and magic. Animals will talk, fairy godmothers will predict the future, tapestries will come alive, riddles will be a life-and-death matter, straw will be spun into gold. And all this will happen in a world of castles, dark forests, farmyards and the hidden places under the green hills.

For Pamela Travers, growing up in Queensland, Australia, in the early years of the twentieth century, the world was nothing like this European fairy-tale world. Fields of sugar cane were her forests. Shells, palm leaves and pieces of coral were her treasures. But the fairy tales of distant Europe occupied her imagination through reading. In those days you could buy fairy-tale books that only cost one penny. Whenever the family went to town, Pamela would buy one of those skinny, green-covered books.

Fairy tales and myths became part of Pamela's way of seeing the world. When she overheard bits of family conversation, whispered secrets, she turned these scraps into myths. The cousin who came to a bad end—Pamela imagined him chained to a mast like Ulysses or having his liver eaten by an eagle like Prometheus. From stories of distant Ireland she imagined a world where poets sang to their harps while heroes cut off each other's heads as veiled ladies gazed on.

Pamela Travers grew up and moved to England. She became a writer of articles, stories and poems for newspapers and magazines. One day, recovering from an illness, she took a break from her usual writing tasks and began to invent a story about a nanny. This nanny, a rather stern and intimidating woman, arrives on the east wind at the home of Jane and Michael Banks. She has with her a parrot-handled umbrella and a carpet-bag full of magic. The story became *Mary Poppins*, a book of silliness, mystery and poetry.

Where did the story come from? All Pamela Travers would say was, "I think that the idea of Mary Poppins has been blowing in and out of me, like a curtain at a window, all my life." Years later, though, a friend of Travers', a poet, said that if Mary Poppins had lived in another age she would have had "long golden tresses, a wreath of flowers in one hand, and perhaps a spear in the other. Her eyes would have been like the sea, her nose comely, and on her feet winged sandals." It was then that Pamela Travers realized that Mary Poppins had come from the world of fairy tales. Is she a goddess? A witch? A fairy? Yes. She is also an ordinary grumpy, vain, impatient, show-offy young woman. For Pamela Travers the world of here and now and the world of fairy tales are not separate. Fairy tales and their people are here with us, and they blow in and out of all our stories.

Anyone who grew up on this continent has had the experience of P.L. Travers in finding folktale settings disorienting. Ask students which fairy tales they know. Ask them to try to remember when they were little and where they thought these stories were taking place. Ask students who grew up elsewhere to bring a story that he or she knew as a small child.

Mary Poppins: A Sneak Preview and Read-Aloud Suggestion

Mary Poppins, the mysterious nanny, arrives suddenly in Cherry-Tree Lane. She comes on the east wind and she leaves just as suddenly on the west wind. In between she and the two children she takes care of, Jane and Michael, have adventures. This is the simplest of plots. Mary comes, she makes magic, she goes. The pleasure of *Mary Poppins* is in the inventiveness and humor of each adventure. This isn't a sit-on-the-edge-of-your-seat book; this is a sit-back-and-sink-into-it book.

One of the magic devices that fairy tales often use is the idea of humans communicating with animals. P.L. Travers plays with and expands this idea in Chapter 9 of *Mary Poppins*, "John and Barbara's Story." This chapter works well read aloud because it is self-contained. It also has a freshness for today's reader because the scene (and indeed two of the characters) do not appear in the Disney movie. The reader (or listener) is therefore free to visualize the action without necessarily seeing Julie Andrews!

John and Barbara are twin babies in the Banks family. In this chapter Travers lets us in on what they are saying. The babies communicate perfectly with one another, with a visiting starling, with the sunlight that works its way across the room, and with Mary Poppins. Why can Mary alone among all adults of the world understand what the babies are saying? This question—Who is Mary Poppins?—is the central mystery of the book. The starling explains, "She's the Great Exception."

In this world everything has a personality. The sunshine is dutiful and needy of praise. The starling is rude, egotistical and sentimental. In this chapter Travers is expressing her own mystical vision of a world in which all things, animate and inanimate, are interconnected and sentient. But the chapter is also very funny as we experience a topsy-turvy baby's-eye point of view. The twins consider adults to be dull, poor things, but easily amused.

The chapter ends with a flash forward of one year, to a time when the babies, having grown up just a bit, have lost their magical ability to communicate with the world. There is a hint of sadness here, but the Great Exception doesn't let us linger. She is too brisk and too busy.

P.L. Travers has written a book that is funny and light-hearted but also makes you think and feel. That's what fairy tales do. No matter how goofy or weird they seem, those old, oft-told stories have a flavor that stays with you. If you hit the right story, it can stay with you for life.

For another baby's-eye view, take a look at Chapter 6 of Ian McEwan's *The Daydreamer*, a hilarious vignette involving a boy who temporarily becomes a baby and describes this experience from the inside.

Mary Poppins makes a good book on which to base a comparison of the novelist's and the filmmaker's arts. This comparison works well with older students, who might be interested to know what P.L. Travers thought of the Disney movie. She liked the animation sequences and she was grateful that Disney resisted the impulse to make Mary fall in love. But she wasn't very pleased with the sweetness of Julie Andrews' portrayal of Mary.

Fairy Tale Writing Projects:
A Classroom Script

Fairy tales are a rich resource for writers. They provide ready-made structures. They are full of haunting images. Their language is polished, memorable and plain. Most important of all, they are about real things. Fairy tales deal with courage, fear, hatred, love, power, injustice, desire, rejection, cruelty and kindness. In our culture we make fairy tales into picture books and pretend that they are kiddie stuff. They are not. Fairy tales are for the folk, the folk of all ages.

A fairy tale changes as we change. One of my favorite stories when I was a preschooler was "The Wolf and the Seven Little Kids." I loved it because it made me feel safe. Like the triumphant youngest goat, I, too, was the smallest in my family and I figured that if things ever got seriously scary I would just hide in the grandfather clock. As a shy teenager I still identified with that small goat, as one who tended to stand on the sidelines and observe. And now I know myself to be that goat because it is he who reports the action and thus saves his brothers and sisters. The seventh goat is a writer, who knows the power of telling stories.

The experience of fairy tales—listening to them and telling them—can be liberating because we own these stories. Fairy tales are not personal intellectual property like novels or television scripts or song lyrics. If someone tells us a fairy tale, it is ours. But there is magic in this ownership, for a fairy tale is a possession that we own more and more each time we give it away. Have your cake, eat it *and* pass it around for everyone else.

Here are some ideas for finding the cake and giving it away:

Make It Yours. Just write down a fairy tale that you know and like. Perhaps it is "Cinderella" or "The Peach Boy" or a Paul Bunyan story. Don't look it up in a book first. Just trust your memory. Write the story down with as much detail as you can remember. Then compare your story to a version in a book. Or try this with a friend and compare your two versions. What did you leave out? What did you make up? Omitting and inventing are the first steps toward making this story your own.

Now live with the story for a while. Read a couple of different versions. Look at some illustrations to the story. Tell it out loud to the kids you are babysitting. What parts of the story really stick? It could be a repeated phrase— "Orange tree, orange tree, grow and grow and grow," "Fee fie fo fum." It could be a character—Raven or the Golem or the Hodja or the rabbit who lives in the moon. Perhaps it is one picture—three drops of blood in the snow, giant Finn McCoul dressed up as a baby, the magic pasta pot out of control.

Write your story again, expanding on all the bits that you really like. Now the story is yours. Sign it. "Hercules by you." "Anansi by you." "The Three Billy Goats Gruff by you."

Switcheroo. Take a minor character in a fairy tale and tell the story from his or her point of view. The ugly duckling grows up to be a swan. Great for her but what about her duck stepsister who grows up to be a plain ordinary duck? What if they meet on the pond one day when they are teenagers, the gorgeous elegant white swan and the little brown duck? When Hansel and Gretel are lost in the forest we know a lot about how they are feeling. But what about the father at home? Perhaps he records his feelings in a diary. When Dick Whittington sends his cat off to sea, how does the cat feel about it? "A sea journey to Africa by Dick Whittington's cat."

Aladdin in Moosejaw. Fairy tales are often set in remote places, in some distant past. But the stories—falling in love, getting bullied, revenge, worrying about beauty, being rejected, tricking the big guys—are all around us. What would happen if Cinderella were in grade eight at your school? What if the fools of Chelm all lived in the same townhouse development? What if Coyote played on your basketball team? What if Jack the giant-killer, Jack of beanstalk fame, Wicked John and Petit Jean were on the same Listserv? And that girl who lives in the penthouse of that highrise apartment? What if one day she let down her long, long hair?

Find a fairy tale that you like and lay it on top of our world. See what happens. Is the big bad wolf a biker? Are three wishes like winning the lottery? Is there a genie on the Internet?

Once you're in the world of dragons, shoemakers, spells and talking fish, who knows where your writing will take you. You might end up on Cherry-Tree Lane.

Fairy tales are not the common currency they once were. Some students might appreciate a refresher course of some fairy tales read aloud. The book list on pages 41-42 provides suggestions particularly suited for upper elementary and junior high. For younger listeners try a collection of shorter nursery stories such as *Ten Small Tales* by Celia Lottridge or *The Old Woman and Her Pig and Ten Other Stories* by Anne F. Rockwell.

Junior high school students often perceive fairy tales as babyish. This idea can be deflected by introducing the concept of folklore, the study of folktales as social phenomena, telling stories not as stories but as examples. This approach seems to liberate the students to enjoy the stories, which they do.

These writing ideas work well with pairs or small groups and with oral composition. One person starts, either orally or on paper, and passes along the story to the next writer/teller.

Once Upon a Time and Beyond:
Books Based on Folklore

Bodger, Joan. *Clever-Lazy*. Clever-Lazy is like all the smart girls in fairy tales rolled into one. Bored by sweeping, she thinks up the vacuum cleaner; impatient with arithmetic, she invents the abacus. Matches, the compass, fun-house mirrors, the kaleidoscope—ideas spring from her head. However, her invention of gunpowder causes some complications. Buoyant fantasy from one of Canada's most esteemed storytellers.

Ellis, Sarah. *Back of Beyond*. What if selkies, brownies, goblins and other beings of the fairy world were among us here and now, in the world of soccer practice, the Internet, babysitting and school? In these stories they are. Lots of room for the reader to decide what really happened.

King, Thomas. *A Coyote Columbus Story*. Illus. William Kent Monkman. Coyote is the legendary trickster hero of the First Nations peoples. In this story she is also a baseball-playing, hightop-wearing girl who just wants to have fun. Thomas King invents a character who is both totally off the wall and oddly familiar. This is a funny, cheeky book with an entirely distinctive voice. It will provoke discussion.

Levine, Gail Carson. *Ella Enchanted*. Wicked stepsisters, Prince Charming, a fairy godmother. This story seems familiar but it is given an entirely new spin in this funny, inventive tale of a girl who is cursed to be always obedient.

Maguire, Gregory. *The Dream Stealer*. The magnificent firebird; Baba Yaga, the witch with her iron teeth; Vasilissa the beautiful. Maguire works these famous Russian folktales into a story of two children who have to save their village from a terrible threat. A good read-aloud.

McKinley, Robin. *Beauty*. McKinley takes the bare bones of the Beauty and the Beast story and fleshes out the characters into real, believable people and the events into recognizable, even familiar situations. Wonderful for those with a taste for romance.

Napoli, Donna Jo. *The Magic Circle.* We can imagine what it is like to be Hansel or Gretel, abandoned and afraid. But what about the witch? What is her story? This book paints a convincing portrait of the woman who lives in the gingerbread house.

Skurzynski, Gloria. *What Happened in Hamelin.* What did happen in those fateful weeks leading up to the horrible day when the Pied Piper of Hamelin lured away a whole village full of children, never to be seen again? Who was this stranger? What was his power? And how did it feel to be one of the children? This story, written with the suspense of a mystery, provides fascinating and spine-tingling answers.

Tomlinson, Theresa. *The Forestwife.* In the Robin Hood legends Maid Marian is usually the person being rescued. In this story the author imagines what it would be like if Marian were the one who did the rescuing.

Yolen, Jane. *Passager, Hobby* and *Merlin.* Jane Yolen borrows from the many stories about King Arthur and Merlin to create the Young Merlin trilogy, a trio of novels about the boyhood of a man who was born to be a master wizard. For the younger reader.

Clip and Write:
Monica Hughes

"You have a grasshopper mind." So the little girl Monica was told by her grandmother. Her grandmother was not paying Monica a compliment, but she had put her finger on the truth. Monica did have a grasshopper mind—lively, energetic, interested in practically everything—a mind that loved hopping from one idea to another making connections.

Luckily for her (and for readers), Monica grew up to be a writer, a job ideally suited to grasshoppers. Ancient history, Norse mythology, cavemen, comets, the moon, undersea life, urban disasters, pioneers, viruses, immigration, the environment, unemployment, genetics, technology. All these interests have found their way into the novels of Monica Hughes, stories of real recognizable people in situations that could only have been invented by a grasshopper mind.

One of the places where Monica Hughes the grasshopper hops is in newspapers. She reads the paper with scissors in hand and collects clippings—"anything that's interesting, anything that may in some future day a hundred years from now be an idea for a story—or perhaps be a linkage."

One day she was hopping through her clippings collection and came across a story of a boy, David, who suffered from a damaged immune system. This meant that he had to live in a completely sterile environment, in a room by himself with no physical contact with any human. This description led Monica Hughes to ask herself, since he has never known any other life, would David be lonely, or would being alone be a perfectly normal way for him to live?

From that question she went on to create a situation in which she could explore the theme of loneliness. She needed isolation; she chose a distant planet, Isis. The setting and its inhabitants turned out to be so rich in story possibilities that Hughes wrote three books, the Isis trilogy, all from the modest beginnings of a single newspaper clipping.

 The Keeper of the Isis Light deals with classic teenage dilemmas, such as personal appearance. It is very suitable for grades six to eight.

The Keeper of the Isis Light: A Sneak Preview and Read-Aloud Suggestion

Olwen Pendennis is sixteen years old. She lives on the planet Isis with her Guardian and her pet, Hobbit. The planet is beautiful, and Guardian is patient, loving and generous. Olwen has almost total freedom and she is important. She is the keeper of the Isis light, relaying scientific information back to earth. It is all she has ever known. Lonely? She doesn't know the meaning of the word. But then the settlers arrive—a colony of people fleeing the pollution and overcrowding of earth, people who force Olwen to see herself through the eyes of others. Loneliness and sorrow enter her life.

The first hint of what effect the settlers will have on

Olwen's life comes as Olwen sits high in her mountain home, under the Isis sun Ra, watching the settlers' space ship land in the valley below. This scene, the first half of Chapter 2, is beautifully constructed. With Olwen we observe individual details of the landing, but because she is looking through binoculars, we don't see the whole picture at once.

This choppiness parallels the emotional mood of the scene. Olwen experiences a range of feelings from excitement to curiosity to impatience to something she has never felt before—a sense of longing. She does not have the whole picture. Neither do we, the readers.

This scene is one example of Monica's Hughes' skillful delineation of character and emotion. *The Keeper of the Isis Light* is in some ways an adolescent romance, and one of its pleasures lies in recognizing feelings that we have all had.

Another pleasure, likely to appeal to readers with a taste for fantasy and speculative fiction, lies in the sheer inventiveness of Isis—the birds, plants, weather, Olwen's bedroom, a world with two moons. Isis feels both familiar and strange.

A third pleasure, especially delightful to writers, lies in the book's structure. Isis is structured around three surprises. One involves Hobbit, one involves Olwen and one involves Guardian. Each surprise makes you stop and look back over the book and think about the story in new ways. When you read it a second time you notice the hints that Monica Hughes has tucked into the story. Which is better, reading or re-reading? Try it and see.

What Did Monica Hughes Read?

When she was young, Monica Hughes had a taste for stories of derring-do with exotic settings. She read such adventure classics as Jules Verne's *Twenty Thousand Leagues Under the Sea*, Anthony Hope's *The Prisoner of Zenda*, Robert Louis Stevenson's *Treasure Island* and Alexandre Dumas's *The Count of Monte Cristo*.

Like many children, Monica found a refuge in books when things were difficult:

> *We moved from Cairo to London and then to Edinburgh, and I found Edinburgh a sad grey city until I discovered the Carnegie Library. Curled up in the corner of the top flight of stairs in our tall granite house, I found the Hero, the Quest, the Sacrifice; I was part of high adventure on tropical islands, breathless intrigue in Europe, time machines and voyages under the sea. Through books the world was mine!*

Monica also discovered early in her reading the delights of narrative innovation, of playing with the conventions of time and space. She remembers first encountering the notion of time travel in a book called *The Amulet* by E. Nesbit. This story of four children who discover a magic device that enables them to travel to ancient Egypt, Babylon and Atlantis so captured Monica's imagination that she combed local secondhand stores, hoping for a magic time-travel device of her own. Of course, she eventually found such a magic route to other times and places—the magic of writing fiction.

Writing Ideas from Found Stories: A Classroom Script

Reading like a writer makes perusing the newspaper a whole new experience. Sometimes the headline stories suggest fictional possibilities but more often, especially for the young writer, inspiration comes from the fillers, from the small oddities that fill in the extra space between crime, taxes and politics.

Sometimes these small items give you a plot nicely served up on a platter:

> *Honolulu. A sixteen-year-old boy was found alive in a ravine six days after he fell 100 meters from a scenic lookout while climbing over a railing to get a better view. Gabriel Robinson was rescued by helicopter and taken to hospital in fair condition. He survived on only water from a stream. His parents thought he was staying with friends.*

What would it be like to be that hungry? How would you try to survive? What if you encountered animals? What would you think about during those six days?

> *School Bars Teen for Wearing Dress*
> *The six-foot, 220-lb. seventeen-year-old thought he would have a bit of fun by wearing a dress to his high school's semi-formal dance. Instead he was barred from the event by school administrators and suspended for three days. "I went out and bought a nice dress," he said. "I was going to have my hair professionally done, my makeup professionally done, my nails done. I even planned to shave my legs."*

How would everyone at school react to the suspension? What if all the students decided to support the rights of guys to wear dresses? What kind of civil disobedience could ensue? What if all the boys declared themselves Scottish and started wearing kilts in solidarity?

> *A British women who was given brain surgery in*

1979 for epilepsy has lost her sense of fear, say researchers. The operation has impaired her ability to respond to negative emotions or detect emotions in people's voices and facial expressions. She finds it difficult to understand TV programs where the plot involves fear or danger and she tends to shrug off personal dangers with a laugh.

What would it be like to not be afraid of anything? Try making a list of your fears and then imagine yourself without them. Would you feel strong and free and able to do things that nobody else can do? Or would you feel lonely and cut off from other people because you are so different?

Newspapers that carry detailed obituaries are a wonderful resource. A man dies at age ninety-five, and the paper gives a brief summary of his life. He was a poor beggar child in England who was sent over to Canada for a better life on a farm. The obituary then describes one incident from this time:

> *Once, while picking apples he fell and broke his arm. His employers put him on a train for Toronto. He had to get off at Union Station and ask the way to the Sick Children's Hospital—and then walk there with the bone protruding from his arm. He was twelve years old.*

From that one small story we can imagine a whole life of poverty, neglect and courage.

Sometimes newspaper stories give you a single incident that could be part of a larger story:

> *About 100,000 pagers rang wild across the United States yesterday. The half-hour beeping spree was caused by a single wrong number punched into a*

computer system. A new customer was mistakenly
given as his P.I.N. a code used to send news head-
lines. When that P.I.N. was activated it triggered
beeps and messages all across the country.

What would happen if a similar error caused everybody to
get the same message at the same time? What would it be
like to be on a bus and have twenty-seven beepers all go
off simultaneously? Could some hacker pull this off as a
practical joke? What kind of person would do that, and
why?

Often newspapers give you great ideas for character,
especially for minor characters:

Say goodbye to hello. "Heaven-o!" has become the
official greeting in Kingsville, Texas. Leonso
Canales, a local flea market operator, has been pro-
moting "heaven-o" for years because he finds
"hello" too negative. "I see hell in hello. It's dis-
guised by the o, but once you see it, it will slap you
in the face." In a unanimous resolution county com-
missioners embraced the new greeting as a "symbol
of peace, friendship and welcome."

What's next, Mr. Canales? When you go to the beach do
you collect "sheavens?" When you visit Finland do you go
to "Heavensinki?"

Need a workaholic somewhere in your story? Try—

When a partner in a Canadian law firm recently
went into labor, she had a fax machine hooked up
in the delivery room. It continued to spew out doc-
uments about an important deal she was brokering
while she was in labor and after her baby was born.

Need some weird parents?

Last year in Sweden, a couple was fined $735 for naming their son Brfxxccssmnpccclllmmmmnprxvcl-mnckssqlbb11116 (pronounced Albin). They are surrealists, says Parade magazine, and wanted their offspring to have a name that was "full of meaning and typographically expressionistic."

Sometimes newspaper articles simply provide a jumping-off place for your own ideas:

Police investigate the suspicious death of a goat running for mayor in a northeastern Brazilian town. Frederico the goat had been leading in opinion surveys in Pilar since his owner launched the animal on the campaign trail in the municipal elections.

What about a student council election where an animal runs? What about a place where the rulers are animals? What do our government and politics look like from your dog's point of view?

Camels are fitted with tail lights in the Australian tourist town of Broome. The beasts, which carry tourists for sunset rides along the beach road, posed an unacceptable hazard to traffic. Tour operators agree to outfit their camels' rear ends with flashing, battery-operated bicycle lights.

What if pedestrian traffic got so heavy in cities that people had to wear turn signals and stay in lanes? What if you had to pay for a parking meter just to sit on a park bench? What if people started turning into cars?

This month Alexander Pollock of Detroit was given a U.S. patent for a rocking-chair design that has space in its seat for a concertina; rocking fills the bellows and the occupant plays the keys with either hand.

What are the musical possibilities of other items of furniture?

The newspaper can also provide gentle warnings for writers against taking themselves too seriously!

Rachel Simon, an author, is making public appearances for her last book while wearing a dress filled with ink that sloshes around as she walks. "It's as if my body is an inkwell," she says, adding that the dress makes her feel less nervous in front of an audience.

 This writing project is particularly suited to small group collaboration. Put two clippings together and see what results.

Swimming in a Sea of Stories:
Novels Based on News Events

Bell, William. *Forbidden City.* A Canadian teenager visits Beijing at the time of the Tian An Men massacre.

Dickinson, Peter. *Eva.* Eva is the first of her kind, a thirteen-year-old girl living inside a chimpanzee's body. A highly original novel with some provocative things to say about overpopulation and humankind's assumptions of superiority.

Ho, Minfong. *The Clay Marble.* The author writes from her own experience to tell us the story of a twelve-year-old Cambodian girl who becomes a refugee.

Hughes, Monica. *Invitation to the Game.* Imagine a society in which there is no work for those graduating from high school. Where will these young people find a sense of purpose, challenge, accomplishment and identity? In this science-fiction novel, they find it in "The Game."

Katz, Welwyn Wilton. *Whalesinger.* A fantasy novel in which a young woman communicates telepathically with a mother gray whale, this ambitious book also draws on the big news headline of 1579, when Sir Francis Drake visited the coast of California.

Mahy, Margaret. *The Other Side of Silence.* Hero, a child who does not speak but is a gifted observer, discovers the secret of the house next door and what it contains.

Marineau, Michèle. *The Road to Chlifa.* The experiences of a young Lebanese man who leaves his war-torn country for Canada.

Temple, Frances. *Taste of Salt.* Contemporary war and conflict form the raw material for this novel about seventeen-year-old Djo, a young man caught up in the conflict in Haiti.

Summers on the Lake:
Arthur Ransome

Arthur, a boy growing up in the north of England one hundred years ago, lived for summer holidays. Like many children then and now, he hated school. He was sent to a boys' boarding school from age nine to thirteen, and it was a horrible experience. Friendless and lonely, he was so hungry for affection that one day when the principal's wife kindly patted him on the head, he had to run away to the bathroom to cry with gratitude.

Arthur was near-sighted but nobody paid enough attention to him to notice and get him glasses. His bad eyesight made sports a misery. Soccer, cricket, boxing—to Arthur sports meant balls and blows that came out of nowhere to hurt and humiliate him. The principal called him a coward and the other boys teased and jeered.

It was a painful time but Arthur hung on every year just waiting for summer holidays. He would arrive home to join in the rush of packing and then the whole family would crowd into the horse-drawn cab that took them to the train to England's Lake District. At the station they were met by a farmer's cart that eventually deposited them at their summer place, a farm beside a lake. Arthur would race around to check that everything was still there and unchanged—the rock-climbing rock, the cowshed and hayloft, the orchard, the butter churn and grandfather clock, the manure pile and outhouse and, most important of all, the lake with its dock, harbor and boats. Arthur would dip his hand into the water to prove to himself that he had really arrived.

There followed a summer of fishing and exploring, of making friends with farm animals and collecting caterpillars, of harvesting hay and making butter, of having picnics and learning how to handle a rowboat. During these weeks Arthur was, as he later described it, "free in paradise."

Some thirty years later Arthur spent another summer in paradise, on the same lake. By this time he was a large, bald, middle-aged man with a huge moustache. He was Arthur Ransome, a respected journalist. He had lived in Russia and reported on politics, war and revolution. He was a busy man working hard to make a living. But one summer he took a holiday. That summer he shared in the purchase of two sailing dinghies with some family friends, Mr. and Mrs. Altounyan and their five children. He spent the summer teaching the children how to sail. Summer ended and the family went home, but Arthur Ransome kept on sailing:

> I sailed and I fished and I landed on islands and made my tea and sailed again and I thought of a camp of years ago on the best of islands . . . . The wind dropped early that day and I was a long time sailing home. But before I got home I had the beginning of a book in my head and I took a sheet of paper and began to put down the things that happened.

With the long-ago memories of his boyhood holidays and his recent memories of a sailing summer, Arthur

Ransome started writing. The real Altounyans became the fictional Walkers and the "things that happened" turned into a novel. Ransome wrote furiously and with great enjoyment:

> *I used to wonder what was going to happen and how, and while I was writing things came tapping out on the paper that used to make me get up and walk about and chuckle as if someone were telling me the story instead of me writing one for other people.*

This book became *Swallows and Amazons*, and it changed Arthur Ransome's life. He was finally writing what he really wanted to write. He eventually gave up his job as a journalist and devoted himself to children's books. *Swallows and Amazons* was the first of what came to be a dozen books featuring the Walker family and their friends. Hundreds of thousands of readers have shared their holidays.

What Did Arthur Ransome Read?

Arthur Ransome liked to read true-life accounts of sailing, such as *The Falcon on the Baltic* by E.F. Knight or *First Crossing of Greenland* by Fridtjof Nansen. One of his favorite real-life adventure stories was *Sailing Alone Around the World* by Joshua Slocum. He admired this book so much that he said, rather fiercely, "Boys who do not like this book ought to be drowned at once." Arthur Ransome was also inspired by the classic castaway tale of *Robinson Crusoe* and the pirate adventure *Treasure Island*. The book he called "the greatest of all books ever written" was Herman Melville's famous whaling saga, *Moby Dick*.

Arthur Ransome doesn't work well in small excerpts or if you rush. Slow down and give the students a nice large chunk at a time. Read Ransome aloud to grades four to seven.

Swallows and Amazons: A Sneak Preview and Read-Aloud Suggestion

John, Susan, Titty and Roger Walker are staying on a farm for the summer holidays, a farm near a lake, a lake with an island. One day the children are looking at the island through a telescope and they come up with a perfect idea:

> *It was not just an island. It was the island, waiting for them. It was their island. With an island like that within sight, who could be content to live on the mainland and sleep in a bed at night?*

So off they go, by themselves, with tents, food, books, blankets, cooking pots and parental approval, sailing in their boat the *Swallow*.

The appeal of *Swallows and Amazons* is two-fold. Its first lure is the huge amount of freedom that the children experience. Off on your own, day and night, constructing shelters, navigating a boat, cooking all your meals, all without adult presence or supervision—this must have been unusual even for children in 1930 when the book was first published. Today, in a world of hourly cell-phone check-ins with parents, it seems like a fabulous wish-fulfillment fantasy.

Equally appealing is the serious respect that Ransome has for his characters. The whole story is one long imaginative game, but the Walkers don't have toys. All the objects they use—cooking pots, sails, tents, a barometer—are real and minutely described by Ransome. Want to know how to pitch a tent on rocky terrain, how to fish, how to navigate at night? Arthur Ransome loved showing people practical things, and this pleasure shows in his writing.

In Chapter 4, "The Hidden Harbour," the children set up their camp for the first time. They explore the territory, pitch their tents, light a campfire and discover a safe harbor for the *Swallow*. The pace is leisurely and detailed; the style crystal-clear. If you want to know the advantages of "skulling from the stern," Ransome is your man. Character, emotion, even plot happen just below the surface. Ransome pays his characters and his readers the rare compliment of treating them as knowledgeable and competent beings. This assumption of competence is balanced by his obvious pleasure in fantasy and imagination. The Walker children rename themselves, defend their island against a surprise attack, perfect their revenge techniques, find buried treasure, expose a pirate and devise a method for communicating with the natives. There probably is no children's book that is so delightful a combination of real work and real play.

Ransome often appeals to the technically minded. As a short writing exercise ask students to think of some physical thing that they know how to do (change a bicycle tire, do the butterfly stroke, make pastry) and to describe this process so clearly that readers could then do the task themselves.

Writing About Summer: A Classroom Script

September comes. You go back to school. Your first assignment is to write a two-hundred-word essay on what you did on your summer vacation. Sigh. You begin.

This summer I went to camp. We had swimming,

canoeing, crafts, skits, campfire and a night hike.
Our cabin was called The Woodcraft Babes.

Twenty-four words. One hundred seventy-six to go. Blink, blink, blink goes the cursor on the screen, waiting for those one hundred seventy-six words.

This doesn't have to be boring. Holidays can be a perfect thing to write about, but not if you approach it like a police report. Cut yourself some slack.

Concentrate on Something Small. Instead of describing camp in general terms, pick one moment or incident and write down everything you can remember. You woke up one night and moonlight was coming in the window of your cabin. All the other Woodcraft Babes were asleep. You listened to all that breathing. What else could you hear? It was hot. You turned your pillow over to the cool side. You kicked the sheet up into the air and then let it settle down on you, making your knees into mountains. You imagined the dreams of your cabin mates floating around in the moonlight like clouds, mixing and mingling. What were those dreams?

One barbecue, meeting a cousin you've never met before, first dive off the high board, the personality of the cat that you were cat-sitting, your drum teacher, making jam or installing shocks on your mountain bike or designing a Web page or house-training a puppy. Pick one thing and be there, totally.

Invent. Embroider, exaggerate, lie. When Arthur Ransome wrote about the summer on the lake, he invented a family for his adventures. He tinkered with reality, merging the events of several summers into one. He shaped the facts into fiction.

If your summer doesn't seem that exciting, think of it as a lump of Plasticene. The facts are the lump. But you can shape it. You can make that lump into a bowl or a snake or a dragon.

Like Ransome you can take a place you know well and put some made-up people in it. Or you can take your real self and the people you know and put them in some imagined setting. If you didn't get a chance to go to a dude ranch or to Hawaii or bungee-jumping, just do it in your head.

> *I'm poised on the edge of the bridge. The harness around my ankles makes them feel as though they are being gripped. There is a slight breeze. Way off in the pale blue sky is the vapor trail of a jet. I take a deep breath and look down to the dark water far below. A bird flies underneath me. Is falling like flying? I swallow and tip my body off into the deep air.*

What then? Imagine it.

Writing down one moment, one event, or even just one feeling might lead you to a poem. Or it might become part of a story. You might write the story now or years from now. Or your writing could just be a snapshot in words. You can take it out in the dead of winter and be there again, inside the summer, free in paradise, on holidays.

Long Days: Books About Summer

Creech, Sharon. *Absolutely Normal Chaos*. For Mary Lou, summer brings a man of mystery in her visiting cousin, a new perspective on Alex the basketball star, disillusionment with her best friend Beth Ann, a visit to her strange relatives in the country and several large surprises.

Curtis, Christopher Paul. *The Watsons Go to Birmingham— 1963*. Winter holds a lot of hazards for the Watsons. Byron gets his lips frozen to the rear-view mirror. Larry the bully gives "Maytag Washes" (a handful of snow ground into your face). Then there's the flamethrower of death. No wonder the Watsons look forward to summer and their car trip south.

Garner, Alan. *The Owl Service*. Two English teenagers, Alison and her stepbrother Roger, spend the summer in a Welsh valley where they meet a young Welshman named Gwyn. The tensions among the three unleash some ancient powers.

Henkes, Kevin. *Sun and Spoon*. How can Spoon accomplish his very important and secret summer goal when his little sister keeps tagging along? For Spoon this is a summer of loss and sadness, of one big mistake and a lot of growing up.

Konigsburg, E.L. *T-Backs, T-Shirts, COAT, and Suit*. During the summer that Chloe spends with her aunt in Florida, she learns many things—swimming, in-line skating, fast-food cooking, how to make friends with a dog and how to stand up for your right to be yourself.

McKay, Hilary. *The Exiles*. Meet the four Conroy sisters. Phoebe amuses herself racing maggots. Rachel wants a bag of Easter eggs for Christmas. Naomi is deciding what to write on her sister's tombstone. And Ruth measures things. Their parents are . . . confused. But the girls meet their match when they go to spend the summer with Big Grandma.

Paterson, Katherine. *Preacher's Boy*. Robbie admits that all the troubles of the summer of 1899 began with the affair of Mabel Cramm's bloomers. Still, he might have averted major disaster had he not staged his own kidnapping. Robbie sees out the century in style.

Paulsen, Gary. *Harris and Me*. A summer on the farm. Romantic? Not when it involves pig manure, cow-kick concussion, the barn cat from hell, a washing machine that morphs into an exploding motorcycle and Harris, the boy who never runs out of ideas.

Pearce, Philippa. *Tom's Midnight Garden*. Tom and his brother Peter have great plans for the summer, but then Peter gets sick and Tom is sent away to stay with his aunt and uncle in their cramped apartment. It is all incredibly boring until one night when the grandfather clock strikes thirteen.

Rodgers, Mary. *Summer Switch*. Benjamin "Ape Face" Andrews, age twelve, does not want to go to camp. His father does not want to go to his business meeting. Somehow, in the middle of the bus depot, they exchange bodies. It makes for a very unusual summer for both of them and a hilarious read for us.

Bird-Man of the Arctic and Other Imaginary Beings: Michael Kusugak

Moving day. Groan. All that stuff. Clothes and toys, dishes and rolled-up rugs, skis and lamps, the TV and the wheelbarrow. "Why did we throw away the box that the computer came in?" "What do you mean, the couch won't go through the door?" "Don't let the cat out! Oh, there she goes."

For most of us, moving day doesn't happen too often. For Michael Kusugak, growing up in the far north, moving was a way of life. For the first six years of his life Michael lived in the age-old Inuit tradition of traveling. The family traveled by dog-team in search of whales, seals and cariboo. In winter they lived in an igloo, in summer in a tent. The nomadic life is not a life for collecting possessions. The family had only the essentials—furs, weapons and tools. But they also had something that required no space and had no weight, but that was essential to their survival. They had stories.

Small Michael would fall asleep every night to the stories told by his parents and grandmother. Legends, family stories, funny stories, stories with something to teach. He heard stories of the seasons and of the animals he knew— the bear, the cariboo and the little ground squirrel known as the siksik. And he heard stories of imaginary beings—

dwellers deep in the ocean, high in the fall sky or hiding just out of sight. Stories became as much a part of Michael as the food he ate.

Michael Kusugak grew up and his world changed drastically. He went to school. He lived for a time "down south," where he encountered things he had never seen before, like trees and cows. Michael married and settled in Rankin Inlet, on Hudson Bay. He worked as a pilot, a potter and in a college. He had four sons. He told the boys stories. And he began to write.

One year the children's writer Robert Munsch visited Rankin Inlet. He stayed with Michael and his family. The two men went hunting and fishing and they began to exchange stories. Soon they were working on a story together. The story became the picture book *A Promise Is a Promise.*

In writing *A Promise Is a Promise,* Michael Kusugak reached back to his early childhood to a story that his parents told in spring. In the far north spring can be a dangerous time for children as the sea ice begins to break up. To keep their children away from the hazardous shore, parents would tell stories of the Qallupilluit, a witchy undersea creature who kidnaps children. Michael Kusugak invented his own version of the Qallupilluit and put it into a modern-day setting.

In his second book, *Hide and Sneak* (illustrated by Vladyana Krykorka), Michael Kusugak wrote about another imaginary creature of the north. The Ijiraq, a kind of bird-human, is a creature who loves to play hide and seek. He hides little children and they are never found again. The Ijiraq is good at hiding because it can camouflage itself like the ptarmigan, a bird that changes its plumage season by season. In this story little Alashua disobeys her mother, wanders far from home and encounters the Ijiraq.

In creating the Qallupilluit and the Ijiraq, Michael

Kusugak took characters that already existed in the stories of his childhood and expanded them into his own creations. He transplanted them from the traditional nomadic life in which he was born to the world where he lives now, a world of jeans and TV.

Michael Kusugak still goes out to his isolated cabin on the shore of Hudson Bay, to the place of animals and the seasons. He goes to listen, to think and to remember: "When you write for children you have to draw on things that you knew when you were little." But these days he takes his laptop with him.

Kusugak's books are good examples of picture books that work well for a wide age range because of their folktale roots. Read any of them aloud to grades three to six. Just practice saying "Qallupilluit" before you start! Try reading them without revealing the pictures. Then ask students to compare their interior visions with the published illustrations.

Creating Your Own Creature: A Classroom Script

The Qallupilluit and the Ijiraq share with imaginary creatures the world over the fact that they are like humans ... but not. They are familiar, but strange.

Create your own imaginary being. Describe and/or sketch it.

You can begin with a creature you've already heard of—the tooth fairy, Santa's elves, the Easter bunny, Ogopogo, the bogey-man, the abominable snowman, the gremlin that caused your hard drive to crash, your little sister's imaginary friend. Expand and embroider this creature until you have made him/her/it your own. What does it look like? Where did it come from? What does it want?

You can also invent an entirely original creature

cooked up from scratch. To start, try taking an ordinary human being and changing one element:

Size: Tiny people or giants.

Color: Neon orange skin, yellow eyes, green fingernails (we wondered why her nail polish never chipped).

Feelings: The boy who didn't know what fear was, the girl who couldn't feel pain.

Extra abilities: Flying, invisibility, shape-shifting, animal communication, extra-acute hearing, ESP, immortality.

Needs: The man who never slept, the woman who lived on water and air.

Habitat: Underground, undersea, the people of the clouds, sewer-dwellers.

Sketch your creature. Give it some dialogue. Tell people about it. Pretend you are it and write down your feelings and your impressions of the world. Design clothes for it. Draw a floorplan for its house.

If you live with your creature for a while, stories will begin to happen. Does your creature have a problem? Enemies? Does it remain entirely in its own world or does it interact with humans? Perhaps you are the human it meets.

If your story bogs down, don't try to think up more plot. Instead, go back to your creature and hang out with it a while longer. Ask more questions. After all, nobody knows more about this creature than you do. It came from inside your head.

This writing idea works well as a presentation. Students devise a creature and then introduce it to their classmates, giving them an opportunity to ask questions. Answering these questions leads to a more developed and refined character.

Human...But Not

Cooper, Susan. *The Boggart.* An ancient, invisible, mischievous creature is transported from his castle home in Scotland to Toronto. The modern world gives him plenty of scope for creating mayhem. Don't miss the scene in which he becomes involved in a hockey game.

Farmer, Nancy. *The Ear, the Eye and the Arm.* The year is 2194. A extremely odd and hilarious detective agency, consisting of Ear (can hear a bat burp in the basement), Eye (can see a gnat's navel on a foggy night) and Arm (grabs the phone first), gets a call from the general's wife, a call to action.

Kendall, Carol. *The Gammage Cup.* The Minnipins live in Slipper-on-the-Water, in the Land Between the Mountains. Their life is peaceful, safe, steady and—let's admit it—boring. All this changes when they are threatened by their old enemies, The Mushrooms. Unearthing ancient armor, a group of village upstarts leads their neighbors into victorious battle. Who are the Minnipins?

Macdonald, George. *The Light Princess.* To be without gravity, to bounce and leap and fly like a kite, to be always happy and cheerful—this is the gift, and the curse, of the Light Princess. Only when she finally experiences sorrow does she become fully human. A thought-provoking fable from the magical Victorian writer.

Macdonald, George. *The Princess and Curdie.* Curdie is a miner. He knows how to deal with the goblins that inhabit the underground world. But deep in those dark places live horrible half-human, half-animal beings like Ballbody and Legserpent. Macdonald creates some of the most nightmarish inventions to be found in fiction and then makes us care about them.

Mayne, William. *Hob and the Goblins.* Hob takes care of things in the house. "He tidies away abandoned things, like scraps of quarrels or pieces of spite. He banishes small troubles, makes ghosts happy, soothes tired curtains, charms kettles into singing, and stops milk sulking." Hardly anyone can see Hob, but he is a very useful creature to have around. His abilities are stretched to the limit, however, when he has to deal with goblins.

McGraw, Eloise. *The Moorchild.* Saaski is a changeling—half-fairy and half-human. Rejected by the village because she is different and unable to live with the fairies because she doesn't have all the fairy skills, she doesn't fit in anywhere. This moving book is for anyone who ever felt they didn't belong.

Norton, Mary. *The Borrowers.* Have you ever wondered what happens to lost paper clips and thumb tacks and the last piece of the jigsaw puzzle? They have probably been borrowed, by the miniature people who live under the floorboards. The Borrowers have a pleasant life in many ways, but their survival depends on never being seen. (By us, that is.)

Waugh, Sylvia. *The Mennyms.* The Mennym family lives in a large house in London. The grandparents work at home. Father has a night job. They worry about money. The baby demands a lot of care. The teenage daughter is a bit rebellious. They could use some friends. But they don't mix with their neighbors. They can't. They have a secret. The Mennyms are a family of life-sized, animated, stuffed dolls.

E.S.L.—
Elvish as a Second Language:
J.R.R. Tolkien

Once there was a seven-year-old boy who wrote a story about a dragon. When he gave it to his mother to read, she pointed out that you can't say, "a green great dragon"; you have to say, "a great green dragon." The boy agreed but he wondered why.

The boy was John Ronald Reuel Tolkien, known as Ronald, and he was to spend his whole life wondering about language. Like other students of his time he learned Latin and Greek at school. But his hunger for languages went beyond the classroom. Seeing some Welsh names on the side of a truck, he was seized with the desire to learn Welsh, and did. One day, while avoiding studying for exams, he found a book on Finnish grammar in the library. He said it was like "discovering a complete wine-cellar filled with bottles of an amazing wine of a kind and flavour never tasted before." J.R.R. Tolkien was lucky enough to turn this excited enthusiasm for language into his life's work. He became a professor of philology, the scientific study of where languages come from and how they work.

Tolkien's love of language was also the source of his secret life. All the time he was doing regular adult things like studying at university, serving in the army, finding a job, getting married and being a father, he was inventing his own languages. From an early age Tolkien spent hours constructing words and grammar for his private languages. Each language he encountered added some new element to these inventions. After much experimentation, he settled down to inventing a language he called Elvish, a highly detailed language with its own vocabulary, grammar, history and poetry.

The only problem was that there was nobody to speak the language. So, in order to give Elvish a place to be spoken, Tolkien invented an imaginary land called Middle Earth and some good-natured, small, fat, hairy-footed creatures to live in this land. The place and characters naturally led to story. The result was a fantasy called *The Hobbit*, a book that has invited millions of readers into a land of goblins and trolls, wizards and heroic journeys.

For a mysterious introduction to this section, play a recording of J.R.R. Tolkien reciting a poem in Elvish (available on *Poems and Songs of Middle Earth*, a Caedmon recording, out of print but available in libraries) and ask students to guess which language is being spoken.

What did J.R.R. Tolkien Read?

When J.R.R. Tolkien was a boy he liked hero stories and tales of fantasy.

He enjoyed *Alice in Wonderland* by Lewis Carroll, Chaucer's *Canterbury Tales*, *The Princess and the Goblin* and *The Princess and Curdie* by George Macdonald, *Sir Gawain and the Green Knight*, *The Red Fairy Book* by Andrew Lang. Tolkien's favorite story in *The Red Fairy Book* was the tale of Sigurd, who slew the dragon Fafnir. Tolkien loved dragons. In fact, he liked to read books very much like the ones he ended up writing. He once remarked that one of the reasons he wrote *The Hobbit* and *The Lord of the Rings* was because he couldn't find enough of the sort of thing he liked to read. He wrote for himself as a reader.

The Hobbit: A Sneak Preview and Read-Aloud Suggestion

Bilbo Baggins, our introduction to the world of Middle Earth, is a reluctant hero. Being a hobbit, he likes comfort —a cozy house, regular substantial meals, a good night's sleep and maybe, for excitement, a game of darts. How then does he find himself on an adventure involving capture by trolls, escape from goblins, rescue by eagles, and attacks by wolves, giant spiders and a loathsome fire-breathing dragon? It all starts with a visit from Gandalf the wizard who drops in for tea. Somehow Bilbo finds himself agreeing to accompany Gandalf and thirteen dwarves on a quest for the lost treasure of the King Under the Mountain. *The Hobbit* is the story of their journey from Bilbo's home at Bag End through the hobbit lands, the Lone-lands, the fair valley of Rivendell, through the Misty Mountains to the Land Beyond, through the terrible forest of Mirkwood to the Lonely Mountain, home of the treasure and the dragon who guards it. In the course of this year-long journey, Bilbo saves the dwarves' lives many times with cunning and bravery, and becomes a true hero.

In *The Hobbit* J.R.R. Tolkien makes you feel that you are in a very strange place that is also very familiar—a place you might have visited once but have almost forgotten. He achieves this effect with words—ordinary words with a twist. *The Hobbit* is written in English but when you read it, especially if you read it aloud, it is as though you are hearing echoes of some other language. For a taste of Middle Earth, try eavesdropping on Gollum in Chapter 5, "Riddles in the Dark."

Poor old Bilbo gets into tights spots in almost every chapter of *The Hobbit*. At one point he escapes a goblin attack only to find himself lost in a dark tunnel on the edge of a deathly cold underground lake, the home of a slimy creature called Gollum. Gollum is a Tolkien invention, but if you've ever waded through the ooze at the edge of a lake and felt something brush your leg, you have met Gollum before.

In Gollum's first words to Bilbo he refers to him as a "tasty morsel." Bilbo is understandably worried by what this encounter will bring. In the pitch dark and slimy blackness his sword isn't much use to him, and he ends up in a riddle contest with Gollum. Suspense builds as the riddles become more and more difficult. Gollum's polite and affectionate tone becomes more and more chilling, and Bilbo feels more and more trapped. But our stout hobbit prevails, wins the war of words and escapes to the dilemma of the next chapter, appropriately called "Out of the Frying-Pan Into the Fire."

The Hobbit can be read as an introduction to the more substantial and complicated *Lord of the Rings* trilogy, but also works perfectly well on its own. It is an excellent read-aloud for grades four to seven.

Starting Your Own Language: A Classroom Script

Every so often, throughout history, the idea of an invented language pops up. A hundred years ago, for example, a Polish eye doctor, L.L. Zamenhof, had a great idea. He believed that if all the people in the world shared a common second language, it would lead to international communication, understanding and peace. So he invented Esperanto. Esperanto has about 100,000 speakers worldwide, which is quite an accomplishment. It continues to add new words as the world changes. Cyberspace, for example, is *Ciberspaca*. But it did not fulfill Dr. Zamenhof's dream. We have neither a universal language nor world peace.

Will there ever be a world language? Some people, looking at the world of advertising and the Internet, think that language will be English. But English is illogical, quirky and difficult to learn. Esperanto is logical, consistent and easy to learn. Sometimes humans are hard to figure out.

What does Esperanto look like? *Mi mangas ovojn dimancon matene.* I eat eggs on Sunday morning. *Tiu viro parolas al si.* That man is talking to himself. *Tigro estas pli dangera ol kato.* A tiger is more dangerous than a cat.

Do you speak Spanish, Italian or French? Some of these words will look familiar. Chinese or Farsi won't help you too much. That's one of the weaknesses of Esperanto.

A class of multilingual students will have their own experiences of the illogicality of English. A discussion of these experiences can give unilingual English-speaking students a new perspective on language.

A more recent invented language is Klingon, the language of Star Trek. Beginners can easily pick up a few words: child – *puq*, error – *Qagh*, hand – *ghop*, war – *VeS*, peace – *roj*, planet – *yuQ*, eat – *Sop*, surrender – *jegh*, go – *jaH*, kill – *Hoh*, see – *legh*.

But it quickly gets more complicated—just the sort of

complication that Tolkien would have loved. Here's something on suffixes, for example:

Type 2 suffixes express how much choice the subject has about an action, or how predisposed the subject is to doing it: *niS* — need, *SopniS* — He needs to eat; *qang* — willing, *Sopqang* — He is willing to eat; *rup* — ready, prepared (referring to beings), *bIhoHrup* — You are ready to kill.

The suffix *rup* is never used with the verb *ghuS*, which means "to be prepared to launch or project something." If not explicitly stated otherwise in the context, it always refers to torpedoes.

Master all these details and more, and some day you will be able to boast, *"tlhIngan Hol JIjatlhIah"* — I can speak Klingon!

If Klingon looks too complicated, you could always try to master the much simpler language of Boontling. Boontling grew up in a small isolated farming community in northern California called Boonville. The people who worked in the fields, mostly women and children, were bored. So they started inventing their own words. A dollar became a *belhoon*, a cow a *dinklehonk*, a small child a *weech*. These words caught on and after a time everyone in Boonville was speaking Boontling, their own private language. Many of the words were based on the people in town. The doctor had buck teeth, so the word for doctor became *shoveltooth*. A camp cook whose initials were Z.C. made very strong coffee, so coffee became *zeese*. A fellow named Walter had the first telephone, so the phone became a *walter* and a pay phone a *bucky walter*. Some words seem to imitate sound. *Kilockety* is to travel by train; *kiloppety* is to travel by horse. Some words are just delicious little poems in themselves. A party is a *tidrik*. To eat is to *gorm*.

Boonville still exists, but Boontling has died out, which is a shame because it would be fun to take a *pike* (stroll) with your *apple head* (girl friend) down to the local trendy cappuccino bar and order a couple of *horns* (cups) of their best *zeese*.

 Boontling is the easiest invented language for children to understand and will delight grades three and up.

Very few people make up languages as complete as Elvish or Klingon, but almost everybody invents a bit of private language. Little kids make up words all the time, and sometimes these words are so good that the whole family adopts them. Three-year-old Laurel calls the thing at the end of a pencil an *unraser*, and her family calls it an *unraser* for years after. Ask your parents if they remember any words you invented when you were little.

To invent your own language you can start with a single word. Here are a couple of ways to begin.

Like English—But Not. Perhaps your language, like Boontling, will be a sort-of English—English with different words. Like the people in Boonville, you might use people's names. Who's the star player on your soccer team? Tino? Maybe in your language a winning goal is a *tino*. Maybe any kind of last-minute triumph is a *tino*: "Mandy's little brother disappeared at the fair. Everyone was frantic until Mandy did a *tino* and found him visiting the rollercoaster man. She deserves a medal."

Tino could turn into a verb: "His top string broke right in the middle of the fast movement but he *tinoed* the whole thing on the three remaining strings. The crowd went wild."

In which situation would a group of people make up

such a language? They would likely be isolated. Perhaps they are in a space station, a lab in Antarctica, on an island. Perhaps they are in prison. Perhaps they have deliberately chosen to live apart. How did they come to be there? And why do they invent their language? Boredom? The need to keep secrets? A desire to change the world? As a way of getting power? What happens when a stranger appears—a stranger who doesn't speak the language?

A Language for Aliens. If you move out of the world of human language, you can simply make up a word out of thin air. Try it.

gickle

fwinhys

eeeeEeeeeeg

This can be surprisingly hard. If you're having trouble, grab a handful of Scrabble tiles or throw the dice from a game of Boggle. Play around with your letters until you have a word that pleases you.

Your word might have sounds that we don't have in English, in which case you might have to invent new letters or even a whole new alphabet.

p8Olx!

*¥*Ωπ~%∑*

Live with your word for a while. Practice printing and writing and typing it. Roll it around in your mouth. Say it. (How is it pronounced? That's up to you. You are the king of your word.) Try saying it as though it is an insult. Invent a word you would say to soothe a crying baby, a word you would use in a serious technical speech. Is it a noun, verb, adjective? After a while your word will suggest a meaning.

Then comes the really interesting part. Who uses this word? Someone from a far distant past or a remote galaxy? Someone from a totally invented world? Is it a word used by the invisible people who live among us, and to whom we are invisible? Perhaps it is one of the many words for dirt that earthworms have, or maybe it is the word your guinea pig uses to describe the heavenly taste of lettuce.

Your word needs a language to live in, and your language needs some beings to use it. From one word you can invent a whole language. From one language you can invent a whole world.

 An invented grammar, such as that in Klingon, requires some knowledge of language and is best suited to grades seven and up.

In Another Tongue:
Books Using Invented Languages

Adams, Richard. *Watership Down*. Before Richard Adams wrote this long adventure book about the travels of a group of rabbits, he learned a lot about rabbit biology. Then, based on real rabbit behavior, he invented a whole rabbit world with families, friends, villains, disasters, heroes, stories and "lupine," the rabbit language. He helpfully translates most of lupine into English for the reader, but he leaves in a few words to give us the flavor of rabbit life. *Hrair*, for example, is any number above four (rabbits can only count up to four). *Embleer* is the smell of a fox, stinking (used as a swear word).

Deem, James M. *3 NBs of Julian Drew*. "My hand is going 2 WRITE. My hand IS going 2 write. My hand is going 2 write U if it K1775 me." Why is Julian using this odd code in his notebook? Some things are just too painful to write. Julian invents his own language to solve the puzzle of his life.

Rubinstein, Gillian. *Galax-Arena.* "De Vexa lak it effan ya tak risks. Dat turn dem on. An mos of all, dey lak see de pcb die. Sho yo tak care, ya heah? We don wan no wan dyan." What is this language? It is the language of tomorrow, spoken by the young people in this chilling book. Street kids are snatched away to train as elite gymnasts, gymnasts who will entertain...well, that's the question. This is a book where you figure things out as you go along. One of the things you figure out is the language that the characters speak. The more you figure out, the scarier it gets.

Wilson, Sarah. *Good Zap, Little Grog*. Illus. Susan Meddaugh. If there were beings in another solar system and if those beings sang lullabies to their children, they might sound like this: "Yoop dooz, little Grog/there are zoofs in the sky./The glipneeps are jumping/and ready to fly." Illustrator Susan Meddaugh has one vision of zamblots and flumms. You might have your own ideas.

Write While You Sleep:
Susan Cooper

One night writer Susan Cooper had a dream—one of those dreams that is so vivid and real that you wake up feeling as though you have been traveling to some incredible and wonderful place. In her dream she was standing on the roof of a building. Around her was a golden city and, in one direction, a park with spreading green trees. She wanted to go to that park but she could not see how to climb down from the roof. She touched a golden railing, which fell away and became a ladder. She climbed down the ladder and came to a stone staircase. She ran down it, faster and faster, heading for the trees.

Before the dream faded, Susan Cooper grabbed a pencil and wrote it down.

This dream is not what we think of as a story, but it has a lot in common with stories. It has a setting, time and place (dawn in a city). It has details to make us feel that we are there—colors (gray, green and golden), texture (the hardness of stone), and sound (the clanging of the ladder falling). Most of all, it has emotion—wonder, joy, trepidation, excitement and desire.

Some weeks later, Susan Cooper, who was writing a fantasy novel called *Silver on the Tree* (the fifth and final book of her Dark Is Rising series), remembered the beautiful and mysterious image of her dream. She expanded it and incorporated it into her adventure. In one of the most memorable scenes in the book, her characters, Will and Bran, are transported to the Lost Land, to a high roof, from which they look out over a great city. Like the dreamer they descend on a magically appearing ladder.

Dreams feel absolutely real when we are inside them. Susan Cooper captures this same feel of concrete reality in her fantasy writing. The Lost Land is an invented world but it is neither vague nor misty. Will and Bran have magical powers and awesome responsibilities, but they are no plastic superheroes. We know the Lost Land, its colors, sounds, smells. And we feel what the boys are feeling— excitement and fear.

What Did Susan Cooper Read?

Susan Cooper grew up during the war. She says of her childhood books:

> *Sometimes they went into the air-raid shelter with us, to be read by candlelight as a distraction from the bangs and thumps going on overhead.*

Among her favorite writers and books were E. Nesbit, Rudyard Kipling, the Pooh books, Arthur Ransome, Charles Dickens, H.G. Wells and A.A. Milne's poetry.

Silver on the Tree: A Sneak Preview and Read-Aloud Suggestion

In *Silver on the Tree* Will Stanton, who is the last-born of the Old Ones, guardians of the light, wages a final battle against the rising forces of darkness.

Will has powerful friends—the wizard Merriman, Bran, ancient son of Arthur, and all the Old Ones—who

gather at times of crisis. But the enemies of the light have
their own powerful weapons of trickery, mind-twisting
and deceit. As we travel with Will across time and space,
from the building of an amphitheater in Roman Britain to
a Caribbean carnival, from the kingdom of Arthur to a
run-in with a couple of bullies in the here and now, the
suspense never lets up. Demon animals, imprisonment in
a maze of mirrors, kindly adults who are not what they
seem, the horrible fleshless horse of bones—the dark is
rising, now as then, and Will and Bran must save us as
they work through their quest:

> *They must go to the lost land, in the moment when
> it shall show itself between the land and the sea.
> And a white bone will prevent them, and a flying
> may-tree will save them, and only the horn can stop
> the wheel. And in the glass tower among the seven
> trees, they will find the crystal sword of the Light.*

Make sense? It does inside the dream.

Silver on the Tree, in the tradition of heroic fantasy,
grapples with the big questions of good and evil, loyalty
and betrayal. The action moves back and forth between
this world and the legendary world of Arthur's Britain. In
Chapter 2, "Black Mink," the setting shifts from the here-
and-now countryside near Will's home to the magical and
dignified world of fifteen centuries ago and back again. In
the opening scene we see one manifestation of the powers
of darkness in the contemporary world as three bullies
torment a small Indian boy. Will and his brother intervene
and then return home to a chilling scene in which a mink
attacks the chicken house.

Then Susan Cooper, in one of her smooth, controlled,
dream-like transitions, transports Will back to the time of
the Old Ones. The listener will notice the shift in language

that signals this different world. Our world is described in warm, familiar, casual, jokey terms. The language of the old time is more stylized, rhythmical, poetic and just remote enough to signal to us that we are in a world of different dimensions.

 The books in the Dark Is Rising quintet are *Over Sea, Under Stone, The Dark Is Rising, Greenwitch, The Grey King* and *Silver on the Tree.* They can stand alone but have an added depth and richness when read as a series.

 Susan Cooper's language flows beautifully. She is a pleasure to read aloud and appeals to grades six to nine.

To meet some Susan Cooper fans (and to see a beautifully designed Home page) see The Susan Cooper Home Page at http://missy.shef.ac.uk/~emp94ms/

Dream Writing: A Classroom Script

Dreams have fascinated humans since the dawn of time. Some people believe that dreams contain messages about the future. Some believe that dreams are communications from other worlds, from other beings or the dead. Some people think that dreams are a kind of code that can be translated. Others believe that dreams tell us important things about our true selves.

One thing is certain. When we dream we are all writers. We are taking all the stuff that is in our heads and rearranging it to create something that nobody else could have made. And it takes no effort. It is all free for the taking, waiting for us under our pillows every night.

Dreams give us pictures—a tapestry from which people emerge and walk around the room, a keyboard that produces three-dimensional wooden letters as you type, a tiny man with a human body and butterfly wings. Dreams give us new selves to try on—a body-builder self, shiny and muscular; a flying self; a self who smokes cigars; a desperately poor old woman who lives in a house made of twisted wire. Dreams give us crazy jokes like bedsheets with glued-on Smarties, or the museum guard who, when warned that the museum is about to fall down in an earthquake, says, "Never mind, just learn to play the trombone." And dreams give us powerful feelings—the panic of stepping onto a carpet that turns into quicksand, the frustration of trying to buy a ticket for the circus and all the ticket taker will give you is three eggs, the exhilaration of swooping down a steep gravel hill while sitting on a suitcase, the horror of seeing a baby that is only a head.

Dreams start fading away the moment we wake up. Sometimes all that is left is the feeling. Writing down your dreams helps capture them. It also becomes easier to remember your dreams if you start recording them. Keeping a dream journal has two big advantages for a writer. First of all, you don't have to think about what to write. Your subconscious did all the work. Second, dreams give you lots of good stuff. Perhaps you will never use a dream as directly as Susan Cooper did, but there will be something there to enrich your writing—an image, a character, a setting, a weird joke, a question, a feeling.

Dreams are a gift for everyone, especially for writers.

 Keeping a dream journal is an ongoing project. An effective one-session workshop, however, can be based on the question, "Do you have a recurring dream?"

Dreams of Writers

L.M. Montgomery (*Anne of Green Gables*):

One night, when I was about ten years old, I dreamed a curious and rather horrible little dream. I dreamed that there had been a terrific snowstorm and that I was walking to school through a low and narrow tunnel that had been cut through the enormous drifts from our house to the school.

This tunnel had many curves and turns in it. I turned around one sharp angle to find my path completely blocked up by a huge, hideous face which filled the tunnel before me. The horror of the face wakened me.

Another L.M. Montgomery dream:

Dreams are usually very unaccountable. I had such a silly one one night last week. I dreamed I was haunted by the ghost of a hat! Everywhere I went I was attended by a black hat floating in the air beside my head. When I tried to grasp it my hand went though it in the most approved ghostly fashion. I was not frightened only annoyed because of the comment it provoked—since the hat seemed to be visible to all!

When he was a boy, C.S. Lewis (*The Lion, the Witch and the Wardrobe*) had a recurring nightmare about insects. A picture in a pop-up book, of a beetle with moveable pincers, haunted him and he dreamed of insects, "their angular limbs, their jerky movements, their dry, metallic noises."

Robert Louis Stevenson (*Treasure Island*) also suffered horribly from nightmares. He describes waking "screaming and in the extremest frenzy of terror." His father would come into his room and make up soothing stories about talking to the mailman until Louis could calm down.

Louisa May Alcott (*Little Women*) writes to her mother describing an oddly disturbing dream. She dreams she is walking home from the railway station after a trip, when "turning the corner [I] found the scene so changed that I didn't know where I was. Our house was gone, and in its place stood a great grey stone castle with towers and arches and lawns and bridges very fine and antique. Somehow I got into it without meeting any one of you, and wandered about trying to find my family."

When E. Nesbit (*The Railway Children*) was three years old, she was frightened by her older sister who was dressed up for a play as an old woman: "That old woman haunted my dreams for years . . . She bends over me and puts her face close to mine, and I wake with a spasm of agonized terror."

J.R.R. Tolkien (*The Hobbit*) also had a recurring dream. A great wave would tower up and move over trees and green fields, threatening to drown him and everyone around him. When he was an adult he called this his Atlantis complex, referring to the ancient myth of an island that sinks beneath the sea.

Past Midnight: Dream Stories

Browne, Anthony. *Willy the Dreamer.* Willy the Gorilla dreams of all the things the future might hold. Along the way illustrator and master trickster Anthony Browne hides visual puns, jokes, bananas, Alice in Wonderland, and a celebration of the masterworks of western painting. This book is for everyone from kindergarten to college.

Carroll, Lewis. *Alice's Adventures in Wonderland.* In the most well-known literary dream of all time, Alice falls asleep on a hot summer afternoon and enters Wonderland, a world as weird and real as only dreams can be.

Dickinson, Peter. *Giant Cold.* Illus. Alan Cober. A boy, holidaying with his parents on a tropical island, has a dream in which he shrinks, is put on display as an elf-child, escapes on the back of a bird and walks inside the ear of Giant Cold. Like a dream this book keeps you going just to find out what happens.

Jarrell, Randall. *Fly By Night.* Illus. Maurice Sendak. "At night David can fly. In the daytime he can't. In the daytime he doesn't even remember that he can." When David is night flying he can see the dreams of his parents, his dog, a herd of sheep, and he can hear the conversations of mice and a mother owl telling a bedtime story. Is this a book about dreaming or not?

London, Jonathan. *Into This Night We Are Rising.* Illus. G. Brian Karas. In this dream journey the children float, fly and sail through a sky of cloud pillow fights, music, friendly dragons and animals in the stars. This is more like a poem than a story. A few simple words, carefully chosen, can take you to another world.

McEwan, Ian. *The Daydreamer.* Peter is a champion daydreamer. He imagines himself into other beings—the cat, his sister's doll, a baby and, weirdest of all, a grown-up. But what if it all, including the daydreams, is a dream?

Rylant, Cynthia. *The Dreamer.* Illus. Barry Moser. From daydreams and night dreams the artist creates a whole world and lives in it. But who is this artist?

Van Allsburg, Chris. *Ben's Dream*. If you meet a friend in a dream is that friend really there? No, it's just your dream. But what if the friend also has the dream and sees you? This is the puzzle of this story of two friends who float away in a flood.

Van Allsburg, Chris. *The Sweetest Fig*. Monsieur Bibot the dentist receives two figs that make his dreams come true. After the first fig he ends up in public without his trousers, so he tries to hypnotize himself into dreams of wealth. It doesn't quite work out.

Yours Affectionately:
Beatrix Potter

One day in 1893 a young woman named Beatrix Potter had a problem. She was holidaying with her parents in Scotland and she wanted to write a cheery letter to a family friend, a little boy called Noel Moore who was sick in bed. But what do you say to a five-year-old? She admits her problem right at the beginning of the letter:

My Dear Noel,
I don't know what to write to you . . .

But then she invents a wonderful solution:

. . . so I shall tell you a story about four little rabbits whose names were Flopsy, Mopsy, Cottontail and Peter. They lived with their mother in a sand bank under the root of a big fir tree.

The letter continues with the story of naughty Peter who disobeys his mother and goes into Mr. McGregor's garden but escapes in the nick of time.

Beatrix Potter put into this story-letter all the things a five-year-old boy might like—being bad, delicious food, losing your jacket and a chase scene. She also named the hero after her own rabbit, a pet that Noel had met many times. Best of all, Beatrix Potter illustrated the letter with pen-and-ink drawings of the rabbit family, of Mr. McGregor wielding his rake, of the cabbages in the garden and of Peter tucked into bed on his return home.

Noel carefully kept this letter, which is lucky because seven years later Beatrix Potter asked to borrow it back. She had decided to try to publish *Peter Rabbit* as a book. She revised the story by adding a new character, a longer, more suspenseful middle section, more drawings and one colored illustration. She copied it out into a lined exercise book and sent it off to publishers.

Six publishers rejected it.

Discouraged but determined, Beatrix Potter decided to publish the book herself. She paid to have 250 copies printed and she gave many of them away as Christmas presents. The story was so popular that she had to print more copies right away, and the book soon found a publisher. Again Beatrix Potter did some revisions, adding colored pictures throughout. The publisher made 8,000 books, and they sold immediately. Peter Rabbit was on his way.

The Tale of Peter Rabbit has been around for nearly one hundred years. Your great-great-grandmother might have read it. It has been translated into a twenty-nine languages from Icelandic to Latin. There are Peter Rabbit baby clothes, mugs, stickers, figurines, posters, T-shirts and slippers. Peter has been featured on a postage stamp, on wallpaper and on a board game. There is a ballet based on Beatrix Potter's stories and a movie made from that ballet.

And it all started with a letter.

Many famous children's books, such as *Alice in Wonderland* and *The Wind in the Willows,* began as a story for a specific child. For a short writing exercise, ask students to think of a small child they know well. It could be a sibling, neighbor, relative or someone they babysit. List five things this child likes. These could be food (toast fingers), toys (a shark puppet), objects (their blanket), interests (dragons), or activities (pretending to be a dog). Now incorporate these five things into a one-page story.

What did Beatrix Potter Read?

Alice in Wonderland, *The Art of Flower Painting*, *Birds Drawn from Nature*, Edward Lear's *Book of Nonsense*, Walter Crane's *The Baby's Opera*.

Tales of Beatrix Potter: A Sneak Preview and Read-Aloud Suggestion

In her now-famous letter to Noel Moore, Beatrix Potter demonstrates one of the secrets of good letter-writing. She writes of things she cares about, in this case rabbits.

Beatrix Potter had a huge number of pets over her lifetime. When she was a child living in London, she would smuggle home animals from her summer holidays in the country. At one point she had, hidden in the nursery, a frog named Punch, two lizards named Toby and Judy, some anonymous water newts and a fourteen-inch snake called Sally.

Beatrix could have been a lonely little girl. She didn't go to school and she had few child friends (her parents thought other children would pass along germs). Often she had only her younger brother, Bertie, to play with. But her animals provided companionship. They were her friends; she often called them the "people." Beatrix was a talented artist from a young age, and animals were the subjects of her many drawings. A sketchbook that she kept on holiday when she was nine years old includes a detailed painting of various kinds of bugs. Up to the last days of her life she was still putting little sketches of her sheep into her letters.

Beatrix was also very interested in science, and again animals were an inspiration. If she and Bertie found a dead rabbit, they would skin it and boil it so that they could study the skeleton. Once when Bertie was going away, he left Beatrix to babysit his pet bat. His instructions for its care included directions for how to stuff the bat should it die while he was away. A spirit of scientific curiosity stayed with Beatrix her whole life. During one seaside holiday she discovered bugs in her hotel bed. She noted their characteristics with interest: "a very extraordinary creature for all the world like a hairy caterpillar but it hopped." (She did however conclude, after a sleepless night, that "it is possible to have too much Natural History in a bed.")

Animals were friends and subjects of study for Beatrix but, most happily for generations of readers, they were also inspiration for her stories. Following *Peter Rabbit*, Beatrix wrote a tale for Noel's sister, Freda—a mouse story called *The Tailor of Gloucester*. Another sister, Norah, received a picture-letter featuring a squirrel, and this turned into *The Tale of Squirrel Nutkin*. A hedgehog named Mrs. Tiggy, Hunca Munca the mouse who traveled with Beatrix in a specially built mouse travel case, the cats who sat on the wall in her garden, a farm duck named Jemima, a pig who tried to chew Beatrix's boots, a rat who was discovered under the kitchen table—they all found their way into books, nearly thirty in all.

Later in life, after she married and became a busy sheep farmer, Beatrix Potter wrote very few more stories. She said that she was "written out," and perhaps she was just too tired. But she never stopped writing letters. She corresponded with old friends, she answered fan mail, she wrote to children. She wrote detailed letters about her sheep and cattle. She expressed her opinions about what she was reading—Dr. Seuss or a newpaper article about the Loch Ness Monster. She penned a furious letter about the logging of a stand of oak trees and entertained a small American child with a slapstick letter about her two Pekinese dogs chasing a rat around the kitchen.

She tried to please her audience and she wrote about things that mattered to her. Good advice for a letter writer. Good advice for any writer.

Because Beatrix Potter has become such an "industry," it is easy to overlook what a fine writer she is. Master of the short sentence and the short paragraph, she is a model of clear, rhythmical, controlled prose. Her choice of words is bold and playful and her depiction of character sly and subtle. Her stories were revised extensively, and this shows when they are read aloud. The older reader/listener will pick up levels of irony lost on the preschooler, while still responding to Potter's well-made plots.

Novelist Graham Greene, who wrote admiringly about the works of Beatrix Potters, recommends especially what he calls the great comedies (*The Tale of Peter Rabbit, The Tale of Samuel Whiskers, The Tale of Two Bad Mice, The Pie and the Patty-Pan, The Tale of Tom Kitten* and *The Tale of Mrs. Tiggy-Winkle*) and the "near tragedies" (*The Tale of Mr. Tod* and *The Tale of Pigling Bland*).

Precise, accurate and respectful to her readers, Beatrix Potter gives us stories that are as satisfying as a three-course dinner.

Beatrix Potter delighted in naming her pets, and she was particularly extravagant with her guinea pigs, The Sultan of Zanzibar, Mr. Chopps and The Light of Asia. Canvas your class for the names of their pets, past and present, and compile a class pet directory. Ask for stories of how these names were chosen.

Letter-writing Tips from the Great Correspondents

Write As If You Are Talking. Listen to what's going on in your head and then write it down.

Here is C.S. Lewis (*The Lion, the Witch and the Wardrobe*) writing a thank-you letter to a little girl called Sarah who sent him a hand-drawn Christmas card.

My dear Sarah—Please excuse me for not writing to you before to wish you a merry Christmas and a happy New Year and to thank you for your nice card which I liked very much; I think you have improved in drawing cats and these were very good, much better than I can do. I can only draw a cat from the back view like this.

I think it is rather cheating, don't you? cause it does not show the face which is the difficult part to do. It is a funny thing that faces of people

are easier to do than most animals' faces except per-haps elephants and owls.

I wonder why that should be!

Use Detail. A small thing described in detail is more inter-esting than a big thing described in a general way.

Here is Beatrix Potter describing her discovery of snail eggs, in a letter to one of Noel Moore's sisters:

I had to dig up my snails' nest when I left home. I found there were 79 large eggs! It was such a queer nest in the ground and the snail had covered it up with soil. The eggs were white just like the eggs you had for breakfast, they would be just the right size for little mice!

Notice Things, Then Share Them. When Louisa May Alcott took a trip to England in 1865, she wrote home to her father, comparing the sound of train engines in England and America:

[Here] the very engine instead of a shrill devil-may-care yell, like ours, did its duty in one gruff snort, like a beefy giant with a cold in his head.

Trivia Rules! Don't restrict yourself to "important" things.

Here is Rudyard Kipling *(The Jungle Book)* writing to his son about an accident:

I was cutting off a dead branch with my knife (my father had sharpened it only a day or two before on your oil-stone; so you observe all three generations were concerned in the affair) and I drew the blade towards me. It cut the twig like butter and as my left hand was in the light (I don't know why) it cut the forefinger of the left hand from the nail end of the last joint to the middle joint. I don't know what the proper anatomical names are but it was a slash about two inches long and pretty deep.

Be Immediate. Say what's going on right at the moment you're writing the letter.

Here is Lewis Carroll *(Alice in Wonderland)* sitting on the beach on a windy day, writing to his sister Mary:

A mother and child have just passed, the mother holding the child's head as it walks; I suppose to prevent its being blown off!

Here is Arthur Ransome (*Swallows and Amazons*) writing about the view from his window in Aleppo, Syria:

. . . long caravans of camels pass bringing in stone from the desert. Also there are donkeys carrying everything possible, from a chest of drawers to a gramophone, from a sack of flour to a gorgeously dressed sheik.

Doodle, Draw and Decorate. Sometimes drawings make things clearer and sometimes they are just for fun. Grab a pencil or some felts. Check out the graphics on your computer. Rubber stamps and stickers are also good.

Here is Beatrix Potter writing to a girl called Dulcie:

Talking of tails, I saw a most curious sight the other day after heavy rain the hill sides are slippery, and I saw a neighbour's cow tobogganing as if she had been shot out of a gun—she flew down hill sitting on her tail. If she had not kept all her legs in front of her,

she would have broken her neck, but she finished on a flat piece of grass, sitting down.

Here is Lewis Carroll talking about his birthday plans in a letter to a friend called Edith:

And what do you think I am going to have for my birthday treat? A whole plum-pudding! It is to be about the size for four people to eat: and I shall eat it in my room, all by myself! The doctor says he is "afraid I shall be ill": but I simply say "Nonsense!

Here is Arthur Ransome telling his mother about what he is going to do about his sprained ankle:

With much love,
　　　　Your affectionate son,
　　　　　　A.
I am going to wear nautical trousers in future to disguise my thickened ankle!

Say What You Are Feeling. Letters are a great place to get things off your chest. Whining on paper is often preferable to live-action whining.

Here is L.M. Montgomery (*Anne of Green Gables*) having a little moan to her farmer friend in Alberta:

My dear Mr. S.:—
We are just in the middle of housecleaning! . . . For
the past four days I've been scrubbing and white-
washing and digging out old corners and I feel as if
all the dust I've stirred up and swept out and
washed off has got into my soul and settled there
and will remain there forever, making it hopelessly
black and grimy and unwholesome.

Louisa May Alcott *(Little Women)* had similar opinions about housework. Here she is in a letter to her friend Alfred:

If I lived alone I should make the beds once a week,
clean house every ten years, & never cook at all
which would simplify things grandly.

In an earlier letter to the same friend, Louisa May describes her new job as a private teacher to a little girl, Carrie. Here is her description of the child:

. . . a demonic little girl who dont digest her food &
does rave & tear & scold & screech like an insane
cherubim. . .

Letters are also a great place to express your opinions on something you really care about. Louisa May again, this time writing to a friend about the issue of equal pay for women:

I believe in the same pay for the same good work.
Don't you? In future let woman do whatever she
can do; let men place no more impediments in the
way; above all let's have fair play,—let simple justice
be done, say I.

Letter Writing: A Classroom Script

Find a Pen Pal. To find a pen pal by e-mail, check out "K12Pals." Send the following e-mail message to LIST-SERV@SYR.EDU:

Subscribe K12 your name.
Example: Subscribe K12 Peter Rabbit.

Write Letters to the Editor. Have they dropped your favorite strip from the comics page? Are there plans to close your local swimming pool? Do you have an opinion about logging or zoos or skateboarding bylaws? Have your say. Get it off your chest. Make a difference. (Be sure to include your age. Adults are extremely impressed when kids write letters.)

Send Postcards. Write postcards to your friends and relatives when you're away on vacation. Practice micro-writing. How much can you fit on one postcard? Stuck at home? Design and make your own postcards using collage, painting, drawing or photos. Then pretend to be away in some exotic location—Argentina, Egypt in the time of Tutankhamun, Mars. Confuse your friends.

Story-Letter Relay. Start a story in a letter. Leave it at some cliff-hanging point and mail it to a friend to continue. Bounce it back and forth. Just remember, as they say in Theater Sports, "No Blocking, No Wimping." (Blocking is finishing the story so that the other person has nowhere to go. Wimping is ignoring what the other person has added to the story.)

Letters From an Altered State. Write a letter as though you are someone else. Every Christmas J.R.R. Tolkien (*The Hobbit*) wrote to his children in the voice of Santa

Claus, describing disasters at the North Pole. Pretend to be your hamster writing to his cousin, describing his adventures in the hamster ball. Be an Olympic athlete e-mailing home on the eve of the medal competition. Compose a letter from an orphan to the parents he never knew. Write the letter that Rapunzel scratched on the walls of her tower.

Pretending to be someone else and writing in that voice is what fiction writing is all about.

Letters are a great place to combine words, pictures and design. Encourage the use of colored pens and pencils, computer graphics, calligraphy, interesting fonts, the decoration of envelopes and the designing of original stamps. Older students may be interested in Nick Bantock's Griffin and Sabine books, a tour-de-force of gorgeous and mysterious book design.

*P.S. The Thank-you Letter Dilemma

Dear Aunt Linda,
Thank you for the socks. They are ~~nice~~ ~~interesting~~ different.

Sigh.
You chew the end of your pencil.
You think about lunch.
You stare at the cursor on the screen in front of you.
You have to write a letter and you have NOTHING TO SAY. Aaagh!
Do not despair. Help is at hand.
Try writing from the point of view of the socks. How did they feel when the wrapping came off and they were looking at you? Do they like being twins? Perhaps they have strong opinions about feet?
Where is the first place that you're going to wear those socks?

Socks. Box, fox, rocks, locks, knocks, talks . . . There's a poem or a song or a rap in there somewhere.

How will those socks protect themselves from the dreadful sock-eating dryer? What are their hidden powers?

What happens when you introduce your new socks to the other socks in the sock drawer? Are they shy or outgoing? Are the other socks welcoming or snobby?

Aunt Linda is going to LOVE this letter.

Yours Truly: Stories Told in Letters

Ahlberg, Allan and Janet. *The Jolly Postman*. In this inventive book we actually get to open the envelopes and snoop at the mail of the witch, the big bad wolf, the three little pigs and other inhabitants of the world of fairy tale and nursery rhyme.

Asch, Frank and Vladimir Vagin. *Dear Brother*. Brothers Joey and Marvin find a cache of letters in their attic—letters between brothers Henry and Timothy, their great-great-granduncles. We read the letters along with the boys and discover some goofy and sad stories of brothers long ago. What makes this book odd and funny is that all the characters are mice.

Cleary, Beverly. *Dear Mr. Henshaw*. Leigh Botts (boy) starts writing to author Boyd Henshaw as a school assignment, but one letter leads to another. Soon Leigh is letting Mr. Henshaw and us into the important things in his life—his loneliness in a new school, his inventive triumph over the lunch box thief, his anger at the broken promises of his absent father. The happy ending is that in the course of this correspondence, Leigh turns into a real writer.

Hesse, Karen. *Letters from Rifka*. Rifka writes these letters to her cousin in the margins of a book of poetry. She cannot send them because her family is on the run, escaping from Russia to a new life in America. Hunger, loneliness, fear, sickness, bravery, humor and the kindness of strangers. Based on a real-life family story.

Lyons, Mary E. *Letters from a Slave Girl: The Story of Harriet Jacobs*. "Freedom! The word taste like Christmas when I say it out loud." Harriet, an escaping slave, writes letters to her dead mother and others in the margins of an old account book. Through these letters we learn of her despair, hiding out for seven years in a garret, of her loneliness, and of her eventual heroic triumph. The letters are invented, but Harriet's story actually happened.

Major, Kevin. *Dear Bruce Springsteen*. Get a guitar. Get a band.

Get a girlfriend. What better way to deal with a life where Dad has flown the coop and Mom has a new boyfriend? And who better to tell than Bruce Springsteen? Fourteen-year-old Terry sorts things out in a series of letters to his hero.

Marsden, John. *Letters from the Inside*. Mandy and Tracey connect through a pen-pal ad. At first their letters deal with regular pen-pal stuff—school, brothers, sports, music. But odd details emerge in Tracey's letters—things don't add up. Tracey obviously has a secret, possibly a sad and dangerous one, but what is it? Can friendship survive based on illusion?

Ware, Cheryl. *Sea Monkey Summer*. In the summer between grades six and seven, Venola Mae Cutright gets a job, opens a bank account, cures her plantar warts with magic, exposes a consumer scam, fails to identify some criminals and decides to be cremated. We find out about these events in Venola's hilarious letters to her friend at camp, her boss and Dear Abby.

Webster, Jean. *Daddy-Long-Legs*. Judy is an orphan. She gets the surprise of her life when the matron of the orphanage tells her that a kind rich man is going to pay for her college education. All he requires is that Judy write him regular letters. Not knowing his name, Judy writes to her benefactor as "Daddy-Long-Legs." Judy is funny, enthusiastic and honest. Anyone would love getting these letters. But who is the real recipient? The identity of Daddy-Long-Legs gives Judy the second big surprise of her life.

Williams, Vera. *Stringbean's Trip to the Shining Sea*. Illus. Jennifer Williams. When Stringbean and his brother Fred take off in Fred's truck for a summer on the road, they record their adventures in a set of postcards home. The search for the circus clown, the ghost horse, the lizard adoption—reading these postcards makes you wish you had been along on the trip.

Digging Up Stories:
Paul Yee

One of the satisfactions of writing lies in the opportunity
to make use of everything in your life. Everything you
experience, think about, study, investigate, encounter or
invent is potential material. Often the best writing ideas,
like Little Bo-Peep's sheep, appear when you are not looking for them.

When Paul Yee was a university student, he had a particular interest in the history of the Chinese in Canada and
the United States. Paul looked at photographs, searched
out diaries and letters, read old newspapers and long, dull
government reports. He was particularly fascinated with
contradictions and gaps in the material, and he later orga-
nized his findings into several books about the Chinese
experience. Paul was searching for the truth, but he was
not thinking in terms of writing fiction.

Some years later, when Paul came to write a collection
of short stories for young people, he began to think about
the research he had done on the various jobs that Chinese
people had taken when they first came to North America.
He remembered a paper he had written on the history of
the Chinese salmon cannery workers on the west coast.
Two details came back to him. One was a newspaper ad
for a machine called "The Iron Chink." This automated

fish-canning machine had resulted in many workers losing their jobs. The insulting name and the hardship of the men who lost their jobs had stayed with Paul.

The other detail Paul remembered was the fact that the foremen in the canneries, the men who supervised the Chinese workers, were themselves Chinese, and that one of their jobs was to interpret for the Chinese-speaking workers and the English-speaking big boss. Because the foremen were bosses, the workers didn't associate with them. But the big bosses didn't associate with them, either. The foremen were stuck in the middle. They must have been lonely, Paul thought.

Paul took these two bits of history—a piece of injustice and the portrait of a lonely man—and fashioned them into an original story, "The Revenge of the Iron Chink," a wonderful tale of come-uppance. The story is very specific, locked in one time and place and situation. But it is also the universal folktale story of the little guy tricking the big guy.

"The Revenge of the Iron Chink" is one of the stories in the collection *Tales from Gold Mountain*—excellent stories for reading aloud, for discussion and as examples of how the past is crowded with stories. We just have to dig.

Tales from Gold Mountain: A Sneak Preview and Read-Aloud Suggestion

The stories in *Tales from Gold Mountain* appeal to a wide age range. Younger readers and listeners enjoy their larger-than-life folktale characters and their tidy, satisfying plots. In "Rider Chan," a chilling ghost story, we recognize a version of the story of two brothers—one good, one wicked. In "Forbidden Fruit," a tragic romantic love story, we hear echoes of the fairy-tale theme of the ailing princess. "The Friends of Kwan Ming," a slapstick tale of greed and come-uppance, reads like a cautionary tale from Aesop. These stories are excellent choices for a fifteen-minute read-aloud.

For older readers the stories have the added dimension of providing an introduction to the Chinese immigrant experience. Covering such historical realities as the working conditions of the railway workers in "Spirits of the Railway," and discrimination against mixed-race individuals in "Gambler's Eyes," the stories can serve to introduce discussion on such topics as racism, immigration policy, the loneliness of being a newcomer and varied cultural attitudes to family. Hearing the whole collection read aloud, the listener gradually builds up a picture of the historical realities of one of North America's most influential immigrant groups.

Writing About the Stuff Around Us: A Classroom Script

Things From the Past. Look around your house and find an object that existed before you were born.

* a photograph of your parents as children
* a letter that your uncle sent home when he was in Africa
* your grandparents' immigration papers
* the clock that your parents bought in a garage sale years ago
* a cup and saucer that belonged to your great-grandmother
* the home movie from when your dad was a toddler
* your mother's bowling trophy from high school
* a mysterious rusty metal thing you dug up in the garden last spring
* your older sister's teddy bear
* the certificate that your father won for art in grade eight

◆ some dried flowers pressed in a book
◆ a war medal
◆ a locket
◆ the collar from the first dog your mother owned
◆ your father's high school annual

Ask about this object. Describe it. Write down this information in point form. Then write a scene in which the object appears. If you discovered a story to go with this object, your scene might be close to real history. But you might choose to invent a new context for the object. This scene does not need to be a story. It could just be a moment in which the object is important.

Things From the Present. Look around your house and find something that belongs to you, and that you think reveals something about you.

◆ an item of clothing
◆ a poster
◆ a printed e-mail
◆ a diary
◆ a birth certificate
◆ a newspaper clipping
◆ a report card
◆ an award certificate
◆ a stuffed animal

First describe what the object really reveals about you. The pink blouse so nicely ironed and folded means that it was a gift that you never wore because you hate pastels. Now imagine that tomorrow you, your family and all your possessions, except for this one object, are captured by aliens and disappear from the planet. An investigation team that knows nothing about you has only this one object to give them a clue as to who you were. What conclusions do they draw from the object?

Perhaps they conclude that you love pastels and that you keep all your clothing in perfect condition, that you are a meticulous dresser and a tidy and well-organized person.

Exchange objects around the class. Play detective. Describe the person you imagine from the object. Write a series of alien abduction investigation reports. Compare these reports to the owner's own story.

For a rollicking example of mock-archeology, see David Macaulay's *Motel of the Mysteries*. Archeologists of the future dig up our civilization and theorize as to the significance of credit cards, toilet plungers and videos.

A field trip to a museum or historical site can provide a springboard to writing. Suggest to students that they concentrate on a single object and spend some time with it, observing, reading whatever information the museum provides about the object, daydreaming.

One writing exercise would involve imagining the object back in its historical context. Put the dinosaur bone back into a living dinosaur. (What is he eating? What sounds does he make?) Imagine someone using that old-fashioned wringer washer. (Are her fingers wrinkled up like prunes?) What was it like to put on that mask? (Did it make you feel anonymous and powerful? What if you were taken over by the spirit of the mask?) That beautiful little statue of a horse—you want to own it. It would feel so good in your hand. (Who made it? Why? Did they long to have a real horse?)

This project would likely involve a visit to the library to find out more about the Mesozoic era, pioneer life on the prairies, First Nations rituals, or the ancient Greeks. A subsequent project might involve incorporating this information into a story in which you are the discoverer of the object or the object has magical powers or is stolen from the museum. The object might lead the writer into science fiction, fairy tale, mystery, action adventure, fantasy or poetry.

Keepsakes: Books Based on Found Objects

Bond, Nancy. *A String in the Harp.* Peter, a twelve-year-old American boy living in Wales, discovers a strange Y-shaped metal object, a harp-tuning key that transports him into the ancient past.

Buffie, Margaret. *Who Is Frances Rain?* Summering at the cottage, fifteen-year-old Lizzie engages in a bit of do-it-yourself archeology and digs up a pair of old-fashioned spectacles. Through them she sees a world that no longer exists.

Clark, Joan. *The Hand of Robin Squires.* Legend has it that Oak Island is the site of buried treasure. In 1971 an excavation using a submarine camera revealed three chests, a pick and a dismembered human hand. Clark spins this discovery into an exciting story of pirates, murder and skulduggery.

Dickinson, Peter. *A Bone From a Dry Sea.* This back-and-forth story moves between the life of Li, four million years ago, and an archeological dig of today—a dig that is searching for Li and her people.

Hotze, Sollace. *Acquainted With the Night.* A doll, an ivory comb, a flint and a journal. Molly and her cousin Caleb find a hidden cache of objects in an old cottage in the woods. When they are unearthed, the mystery and sorrow of the past seep into the present.

Katz, Welwyn Wilton. *False Face.* Laney's dog, digging furiously in the bog near Laney's home, unearths a small Iroquois mask. With the mask comes a story and a powerful field of energy.

Pearson, Kit. *A Handful of Time.* Under the floorboards of a family cottage, Patricia finds her grandmother's pocket watch. When she winds it, time takes on another dimension.

Taylor, Cora. *The Doll.* When Meg is sick she is comforted by holding her great-great-grandmother's doll, Jessie. But Jessie turns out to do more than comfort.

A Bag of Tricks:
Lewis Carroll

Ladies and Gentlemen! Presenting...the Master of Magic, the Captain of Conjuring, the Prince of Prestidigitation! Would you welcome please, the amazing...ALADDIN!

The audience bursts into enthusiastic applause as a tall thin teenager comes into the room. He is dressed in a long white robe and wears a brown wig. He carries a bag of tricks.

The room is the living room of a rectory in a town in the north part of England. It is early evening on a winter's night one hundred and fifty years ago. A fire burns brightly in the fireplace. In attendance is the large Dodgson family, seven girls and four boys. In the flickering light of the fire, the magician in his costume looks so mysterious that the audience almost forgets that he is their brother, Charles, the eldest son in the family.

"Pick a card, any card." Cards are fanned out before the laughing audience. Coins appear from behind the ears of the youngest children. A magic wand floats in the air. A piece of paper is transformed into a boat and then disappears into thin air. "Now you see it, now you don't."

The performance ends with a waterfall of colored scarves and another burst of applause. Aladdin bows low and sweeps off his wig. The youngest children smile with some relief. Why, it is just Charles, after all. This is the same older brother who sings funny songs for them, who makes up limericks for their family magazine:

His sister named Lucy O'Finner
Grew constantly thinner and thinner,
The reason was plain,
She slept out in the rain,
And was never allowed any dinner.

This is Charles who built a marionette theater and writes plays for it. This is Charles who loves charades and puns and teasing. This is big brother Charles who constructed a miniature railway in the garden, complete with tickets and stations, timetables, snack bars and rules ("Station master can put anyone who behaves badly in prison"). This is Charles the entertainer.

The door opens and in comes the father of the family. He leads them all in their nightly prayers and then everyone goes off to bed. But Charles does not sleep. He can't get his brain to stop thinking. So he gives his brain a problem. This is a conundrum he has been stewing over for some time. He imagines leaving home on a Tuesday and traveling west, keeping up with the sun. Everywhere he goes he asks people (imagining that he speaks all the languages of the world), "What day is it?" After twenty-four hours he is back home, having traveled all around the world and it is, of course, Wednesday. But where, on his travels, did people stop answering "Tuesday" and start answering "Wednesday"? Where does the day begin? Pondering this problem, Charles drops off to sleep. (In 1884 the International Date Line and time zones were invented and that solved the problem. Lewis Carroll would probably be delighted to know that with all the translations of *Alice in Wonderland*, he did, in a way, travel around the world speaking different languages.)

It is years later, a sunny July afternoon. Charles is in a rowboat on the river at Oxford. He is thirty years old. He still has a brain that won't stop, and he has made good use of it by becoming a teacher of mathematics at Oxford University. He still loves gadgets and he has taken up the hobby of photography, a relatively new invention. And Charles is still an entertainer of children. With him in the boat are his friend and teaching colleague Robinson Duckworth and the Liddell sisters—Lorina age thirteen, Alice age ten and Edith age eight.

Charles is shy and awkward with adults, but he is at his best with children. He carries a bag of tricks with him from which he produces candy, toys and puzzles of his own invention. He takes children to museums, art galleries and plays. He invites them to wonderful teas with fancy cakes. But his best tricks have to do with words. Anagrams, puns, funny versions of popular songs, acrostic verses in which the first letters of each line form a word, letters written as poems, letters in mirror-writing, rebus letters in which punning pictures are substituted for key words, postage stamp-sized letters in miniature writing. Charles is a word magician.

The sun shines. Mr. Duckworth sings. The girls take turns rowing, and then Alice asks for a story. Charles reaches into his mental bag of tricks and invents a little girl called Alice who falls down a rabbit hole. "What happened then?" the girls ask. The story proceeds, tailor-made to the audience, changing with their questions and their suggestions. Charles recalls an outing of a few weeks before when he and the sisters got soaked by a rainstorm and Alice burst into tears. This event becomes an adventure called "The Pool of Tears." Charles has lately been thinking about the origin of the phrase "to grin like a Cheshire cat," and a Cheshire cat makes its way into the story. Some parts of the adventure are already familiar to the girls, like the story of the three sisters, Elsie, Lacie and Tillie, who live in a treacle well. The girls smile as they recognize their names in code. Elsie is "L.C."—Lorinda Charlotte's initials. Lacie is an anagram of Alice, and Tillie is from Edith's family nickname of Matilda.

Charles puts in songs, nonsense poems and brain-teasers. He creates a topsy-turvy world where things stand on their heads. He wants to stop so he pretends to be asleep, but the three girls demand that he continue.

Alice, in particular, loves this story. When the day is over she begs Charles to write it down. Charles delivers the girls home and then sits up all night recomposing the story he had invented that day, the story of "Alice's Adventures Underground." Over the next months he writes out the story by hand and adds his own illustrations. Then he gives it to Alice as a Christmas present.

Everyone who sees the little book encourages Dodgson to publish it. A couple of years and many revisions later, he does just that.

When *Alice's Adventures in Wonderland* is published, Charles Dodgson, the shy Oxford mathematician, chooses to publish under the pseudonym of Lewis Carroll. This is the name we remember. *Alice* has become the most famous children's book in the world. Dozens of artists have been inspired to illustrate it, and it has been translated into more than forty languages. It is the favorite book of a wide range of people, from scientists to poets, computer programmers to rock musicians.

Lewis Carroll died one hundred years ago, but *Alice* is as popular as ever. In pulling *Alice* out of his bag of tricks, Carroll performed the most astounding magic trick of all.

Encourage students to join Mark Twain, Teddy Jam and Mitzi Dale and choose a writing pseudonym. Carroll used a family name and an anagram. One short-cut to a *nom de plume* is to combine the name of your first pet with the name of the first street that you lived on. Compile a class directory of pseudonyms.

For the story of another magician-turned-writer, see *The Abracadabra Kid: A Writer's Life* by Sid Fleischman.

Alice in Wonderland: A Sneak Preview and Read-Aloud Suggestion

When Alice follows the white rabbit down his hole, she enters a world where things are upside down and inside out. A mouse tells his life story. A caterpillar lounging on a mushroom contradicts everything Alice says. A pigeon accuses her of being a snake. A disappearing cat gives Alice directions and confusing advice. A turtle sings a melancholy song.

Alice grows and shrinks. She is nine feet tall one minute, three inches high the next. Time doesn't behave in the usual way. Characters use words to mean what they want them to mean. Where there are rules, the rules are topsy-turvy. There is a foot race that has no starting signal and no finish line. There is a croquet game in which the balls are hedgehogs and keep wandering off. There is a trial in which the judge calls for the verdict before the evidence has been given and the sentence before the verdict.

The most upside-down thing in Wonderland is that all the adults behave like bad children. They have temper tantrums. They sulk. They argue over nothing. They tell lies. They throw around insults, blame others for their own mistakes and if anyone annoys them, they threaten violence. "Off with her head," screams the Queen of Hearts. In the whole of Wonderland, Alice, who is the only child (well, there is a baby but he turns into a pig), is the only character who acts like an adult. She is courteous, patient and thoughtful. She asks sensible questions. She tells the truth. She tries to get everyone to stick to the point and be logical.

But it is no use. Alice can't make Wonderland behave. As the Cheshire cat says, "We're all mad here. I'm mad. You're mad." When Alice finally blurts out the truth, "You're nothing but a pack of cards," Wonderland disappears.

Why has *Alice's Adventures in Wonderland* survived? It might be because there are times when our world seems very much like Wonderland. There are certainly criminal trials in which the verdict seems to be decided before the evidence. There are days when we feel nine feet tall and days when we feel about three inches. Politicians and ad writers seem to manipulate words to mean just what they want them to mean. And anyone who has ever been stuck inside on a beautiful day knows just how Alice felt when she was trapped at the never-ending Mad Hatter's tea party.

Another appeal of Wonderland is that it gives us a place to imagine misbehaving. Somebody disagrees with you? Behead him. Is a friend getting the better of you in an argument? Insult her. Are you losing a game? Change the rules. Go on. Break windows, throw frying pans around the kitchen, kick people, chuck the baby across the room and sing him a lullaby, Wonderland-style:

Speak roughly to your little boy,
And beat him when he sneezes:
He only does it to annoy,
Because he knows it teases.

Safe and private in their rowboat, away from parents and governesses and church and the classroom, Lewis Carroll and the girls must have had a great time imagining being really bad. We all imagine this at times, but it is not often a good idea to act out these ideas for real. That's one reason we have dreams and fantasies and stories like *Alice's Adventures in Wonderland*.

There are several ways to read *Alice in Wonderland*. You can happily skate along on the surface simply enjoying the story of one small polite girl trying to make her way through the chaos of Wonderland. But to readers with an interest in math, brainteasers, puzzles and puns, the story becomes more and more interesting as you discover more background.

For example, in Chapter 9, "The Mock Turtle's Story," Alice has just finished a very confusing game of croquet (hedgehog balls, flamingos as mallets, a queen who keeps threatening to decapitate one and all) when she is introduced to the Gryphon. The Gryphon in turn introduces Alice to the sorrowful Mock Turtle. The Mock Turtle proceeds to talk to Alice about his school days. Alice asks what subjects he studied. The turtle answers with a cluster of wonderful puns including "Reeling and Writhing," and "Laughing and Grief." If you know that Latin and Greek were part of the standard curriculum of the time, you enjoy the joke on one level. But since laughing and grief pretty well sum up many a school day, then and now, the phrase simply contains its own delight as well.

Illustrators seem to want to illustrate *Alice* the way actors want to play Hamlet. Salvador Dali, Anthony Browne, Arthur Rackham, Barry Moser and a host of others have created their view of Alice and her world. A good route into *Alice* is to compare illustrated editions. It is particularly interesting to compare the portrayal of Alice herself. Check out libraries for a range of editions.

A Bag of Word-Magic Tricks:
A Classroom Script

Trick #1: Portmanteau Words. Portmanteau words are words created from the combination of two existing words. A portmanteau is a suitcase and, like a suitcase, a portmanteau word is a container. For example, "smog" contains "fog" and "smoke." The idea of blending words has been around for centuries, but Lewis Carroll increased the popularity of the idea by inventing his own particularly weird and funny portmanteau words.

In *Through the Looking Glass*, the sequel to *Alice*, Carroll invents the word "slithy," which he explains as "lithe and slimy." In another of his books, *The Hunting of the Snark*, he combines "fuming" and "furious" into "frumious."

Adopt a Lewis Carroll brain and try a portmanteau word of your own.

Some portmanteau words are sensible and useful, like "brunch" and "guestimate." Some are so familiar that we have almost forgotten that they are portmanteau words— "electrocute," for example.

Other portmanteau words: glitterati, infomercial, beefalo, Muppet, faddict, neatnik, mocktail, lamburger, Chunnel, Franglais, witticism, Motown, televangelist, happenstance, broccoflower, Medicare, scrunch, splurge, twiddle, frabjous.

Look around. Is there something you think needs a new blended word? What if you are feeling hungry and thirsty? Does a person who is both mean and conceited need a new adjective? Would a word for a mixture of ketchup and mustard be useful?

Carroll went in for portmanteau words that were not so much useful as funny. In this case try inventing the word first, and let the meaning come later. Start with a word that you like. This is a good excuse to flip through the dictionary. Here's a good one—"curmudgeon/ a bad-tempered person." Now add part of another word to the beginning or the end. "Soccermudgeon/ a grumpy soccer fan," "Hackermudgeon/ a bad-tempered computer hacker," "Curmudgination/ the state of imagining that everything is horrible." This might not be a word that you ever thought you needed, but it could be the start of a story.

 Try the portmanteau exercise with grades six and up.

Trick #2: Parody. *Alice in Wonderland* is full of parodies. A parody is a humorous exaggerated imitation of a poem, song, character or writing style. When you sing, "I hate you, you hate me. We're a normal family," to the tune of the Barney song, that's parody. When you sing, "On top of spaghetti all covered in cheese," you might not even know that you're singing a parody of "On top of Old Smoky all covered in snow." Stand-up comics who do impersonations of famous people are using parody. *Mad* magazine is a wonderful source for parodies of TV shows, fads and advertising.

Many of the parodies in *Alice* have lost their point a bit with us because we don't know the original that Lewis Carroll was making fun of. But he is such a talented writer of parodies that it doesn't usually matter. For example, Alice recites a poem to the caterpillar that begins:

"You are old, father William," the young man said,
"And your hair has become very white;
And yet you incessantly stand on your head—
Do you think, at your age, it is right?"

"In my youth," father William replied to his son,

"I feared it might injure the brain;
But, now that I'm perfectly sure I have none,
Why, I do it again and again."

This is a great poem of the wacko, slapstick cartoon variety. But it would have been even funnier to Lewis Carroll's friends because they knew the original, a serious poem full of *good advice* about *behaving yourself*. It begins:

"You are old, father William," the young man cried,
"The few locks which are left you are grey;
You are hale, father William, a hearty old man;
Now tell me the reason, I pray."

"In the days of my youth," father William replied,
"I remember'd that youth would fly fast,
And abus'd not my health and my vigour at first,
That I never might need them at last."

Give parody a try. For inspiration think of the parodies you already know. Ask your friends, for example, if they know the "other words" to well-known Christmas carols. Ask your parents if they remember other words to advertising jingles from when they were kids. Ads, TV shows, song lyrics, your school's list of rules, the reader you used in grade one, the national anthem. What happens if you keep the style (rhythm, rhyme, structure, melody) of one of these but change the content?

Parody is particularly suited to group invention and often happens spontaneously, when you're sitting around with friends feeling goofy. Once you start noticing parody, you'll see it everywhere. Give it a try:

"Mary had a little spam . . ."

"T'was the fight before Christmas . . ."
Carry on.

 Adolescence is the great time for parody. Try these ideas with grades seven and up.

Trick #3: Riddles. At the mad tea party, the Mad Hatter suddenly stares at Alice and asks, "Why is a raven like a writing desk?" Alice is relieved. Now she knows what's going on. It's riddle time.

Lewis Carroll was a riddle master. One of his riddles, made up when he was a student and published in one of the Dodgson family magazines, stumped people for thirty-one years!

Riddles have been around for a long time. A riddle was discovered carved on a stone tablet in Babylon. In Greek mythology the hero Oedipus has to solve a riddle posed by the Sphinx of Thebes. Riddles can be plain funny, but they can also have a dark side, used as weapons in a game of power, as in the riddle contest between Bilbo Baggins and Gollum in *The Hobbit*.

Riddles have to make sense, but not ordinary sense. Inventing and solving riddles involves making your brain jump sideways. Sideways thinking is a useful skill for a writer, and making up and solving riddles can put you in a writerly state of mind.

Here are some riddle types to try.

The Pun Riddle

What do vampires have for dinner? Answer: Human beans.

What do you get when you put a canary in a blender? Answer: Shredded tweet.

What did one melon say to another? Answer: "I cantaloupe with you."

Pun riddles are jokes for the ear, using pairs of words or phrases that sound alike or almost alike. To make up a pun riddle, start with a sound-alike pair of words and then work backwards from the punchline. Hair/Hare. Play with "hair"—hairline, hair loss, hair piece, hairdresser. . . That's it. Hairdresser, hare-dresser.

Why did Beatrix Potter put Peter Rabbit in clothes? Answer: Because she was a hare-dresser.

Or take a well-known phrase, change it slightly and work back to the question. Anne of Green Gables. . . Anne of Green Bagels . . . Fan of Green Bagels . . .

What do you call a person who likes moldy delicatessen food? Answer: Fan of Green Bagels.

(This is a space in which to groan, the usual response to pun riddles.)

Word-Breakdown Riddles

My first is in chocolate, but not in ham.
My second's in cake and also in jam.
My third at teatime is easily found,
My whole is a friend who's often around.
What am I?
Answer: A cat.

Riddles of this type are really about spelling and rhyming. Start with a short word and give it a try. How about equal time for dogs? "My first is in dingbat but never in nut . . ."

Riddles About Ordinary Objects

There is a thing that nothing is,
And yet it has a name.

It's something tall
And something short,
It tumbles if we fall.
It joins our sport,
And plays at every game.

What is it? A shadow.

You throw away the outside and cook the inside,
Then you eat the outside and throw away the inside.

What is it? A cob of corn.

This kind of riddle is the Rolls-Royce of the riddle world. Not only do these riddles amuse and fool you, they often have a kind of eerie beauty all their own, the poetry of the ordinary physical world. To invent one of these riddles you simply have to look at ordinary objects with fresh eyes. Glasses, shoelaces, pizza, your nose, a computer mouse, compost, a Zamboni, keys, hail, answering machines, a basketball, the moon, airbags, chess pieces.

Look hard. Imagine being this object. Think of all the places you would find it. Think about its origins and its uses.

Especially think about contradictions. In a basketball game everyone is trying to get the ball, only so that they can throw it away. A pawn is the lowest-ranking chess piece but it can have the greatest power.

Then give us just enough clues without giving the game away.

When first I appear I seem mysterious,
But when explained I am nothing serious.
Answer: A riddle.

The Babylon Riddle

What grows fat without eating?
Answer: A rain cloud.

The Riddle of the Sphinx

What creature walks on four legs in the morning, on two at noon, and on three in the evening?

Answer: Man. He crawls on all fours as a baby, walks on two legs for most of his adult life, and resorts to a walking-stick in his retirement.

Gollum's Final Riddle

This thing all things devours;
Birds, beasts, trees, flowers
Gnaws iron, bites steel;
Grinds hard stones to meal;
Slays king, ruins town,
And beats high mountain down.

Answer: Time.

 Riddles appeal to all ages. Younger students enjoy collecting and telling riddles. Older riddle masters can try their hand at riddle invention.

Word Play: Stories That Play with Language

Fleischman, Sid. *The Whipping Boy.* Characters like Hold-Your-Nose Billy sparkle in this story of Prince Brat (who has enough lip for two sets of teeth) and his whipping boy Jemmy. Short chapters, ample suspense and some of the best insults between two covers make this Newbery winner a delicious read-aloud.

Hoban, Russell. *The Mouse and His Child.* What lies beyond the last visible dog? Is it true that Key times Winding equals Go? And how will this help the mouse and his child on their quest to vanquish Manny rat and become self-winding?

Juster, Norton. *The Phantom Tollbooth.* Travel with Milo to the Land of Expectations, Dictionopolis, the Word Market and the Castle in the Air and meet the Mathemagician, Dr. Dischord, the Undersecretary of Understanding, the Whetherman and the lovely princesses, Rhyme and Reason.

Lear, Edward. *A Nonsense Omnibus.* You probably know "The Owl and the Pussycat." Don't miss "The Jumblies," "The Pobble Who Has No Toes" and "The Dong With the Luminous Nose"—poems from the grandfather of nonsense.

L'Engle, Madeleine. *A Wrinkle in Time.* Three beings from outer space—Mrs. Whatsit, Mrs. Which and Mrs. Who—transport a trio of children from their earthly home to the planet Camazotz, ruled over by the dreaded and repulsive IT.

Mahy, Margaret. *Nonstop Nonsense.* Life in the Delmonico family becomes very strange when Mr. Delmonico offends the word-witch. While waiting for the Delmonicos to settle down, we pass the time with the Wily Flingamango, the Dictionary Bird and others of that Mahyan ilk.

Sandburg, Carl. *Rootabaga Stories.* Did you ever hear about Jonas Jonas Huckabuck who had a job as a watchman watching watches in a watch factory? Do you know the romantic tale of "How Two Sweetheart Dippies Sat in the Moonlight on a Lumber Yard Fence and Heard About the Sooners and the Boomers?" Sandburg turns words into a fireworks display.

Thurber, James. *The Wonderful O*. A pair of dastardly villains invade the peaceful island of Ooroo and proceed to destroy everything that contains the letter O. Cnfusin and chas reign. What can the people do to defend their alphabet and their lives when their world is governed not by the letter of the law but by the law of the letter? Read this one aloud.

Wynne-Jones, Tim. *Some of the Kinder Planets*. Kids named Cluny and Hezekiah. The mysterious alien message, "Save the moon for Kerdy Dickus." A little boy staring down a groundhog hole. The spirit of Lewis Carroll lives on in these stories. Even Alice makes a guest appearance in "Tweedledum and Tweedledead."

Book Breeding:
Kit Pearson

One Saturday morning Kit and her friend Barbara were
browsing through the shelves of the public library. It was
a lazy day. In the background was the hum of library
noises. Someone was reading a picture book to a toddler.
"Little pig, little pig, let me come in." Beyond that was the
rhythmic thwack of a librarian stamping Date Due cards.

The girls didn't notice. They were making choices. Kit
pulled an old friend from the shelf, *The Moffats*. Should
she read it again? There's nothing like rereading. You
know what you're getting into. Or was twelve too old for
the Moffats?

Suddenly Barbara appeared beside her and pulled
down a fat book from the top shelf. "You should read
this," she said. "The kids are just like us."

Kit looked at the cover. Black and white and green, pictures of sailboats, a parrot, a compass, kids around a
campfire. She read the strange title, *Swallows and
Amazons*. What could that mean? She flipped it open. A
map. That did it. Books with maps are almost always
good, she decided. This one was worth a try.

Kit loved *Swallows and Amazons*, a story of a family
of four English children camping out on their own on an
island (for a sneak preview, see page 56). And Barbara

was right. The kids were just like them—kids who liked to be outdoors, tenting, fishing, making campfires. The difference was that the kids in *Swallows and Amazons* got to do all this without any adults around. Heaven.

That fall Kit read her way steadily though all twelve *Swallows and Amazons* books. When she finished the last one she nearly cried. But then she just started the series again. Like many readers before and after, she discovered a particular happiness being inside Arthur Ransome's world. That world got into her head and lived there.

Time passed. Kit grew up. She continued to enjoy Arthur Ransome. She went hosteling in the Lake District in England, where many of the books are set, and the place was exactly the way she had imagined it from the books. She bought her own copies of the books and reread them frequently. Sometimes she imagined what would happen to the characters when they grew up.

Kit had known from an early age that she wanted to write, and after a couple of detours into other careers, she did become a writer. As a writer she was always on the lookout for stories, and one day she heard a true story that really captured her imagination. During World War II, children from England were sent away from the danger of the bombing to live in safer places. Some of them came to Canada. Kit tried to imagine what it would be like to leave your family and your friends, to go and live with strangers, and to have to be away for years. It sounded lonely and frightening.

Hearing about these children started Kit on one of her imaginings about the characters in the Ransome books, and what happened to them beyond the back cover. She did some quick math. If Bridget, the baby in the family, had grown up to be twelve years old. . . it would be, what year? . . . 1940. Exactly the time that the English children were evacuated. What if Bridget came to Canada, along with the other Swallows and Amazons?

These questions took their time to be answered. Kit wrote two other books. But then, with her third book, Kit tackled her long-simmering idea. In *The Sky Is Falling*, Norah and her small brother are sent away from their home and parents in England to live with a family in Toronto during World War II.

Is Kit Pearson's Norah really Arthur Ransome's baby Bridget grown up? No. Books have a way of taking their own shape while you write them. *The Sky Is Falling* is not a sequel to Arthur Ransome. Norah is an original character. But the story owes its existence to that moment in the library when Kit Pearson found the perfect book.

If you happen to be an Arthur Ransome fan there are a few hints in *The Sky Is Falling* just for you. Norah's older sister is called "Tibby"—almost like "Titty" in the Ransome books— and Norah's father is called Arthur. And guess which book Norah finds to read when she first comes to Canada?

The Sky Is Falling: A Sneak Preview and Read-Aloud Suggestion

When Norah and her brother Gavin arrive in Canada, they are taken in by the Ogilvies—stern Aunt Florence and her grown daughter, Aunt Mary. The Ogilvies are wealthy and the house is grand. Gavin appears to settle in happily, but Norah is miserable, lonely and ill at ease.

In Chapter 19 Norah decides to run away. In the previous chapter Aunt Florence becomes very angry with Norah and says some devastating things. Norah has reached the end of her rope. She packs, sneaks out of the house and heads toward the train station, with no real plan except to try to retrace her steps back home to England and her family. Midway through her scheme, however, she has a crisis of conscience about leaving Gavin behind.

Norah's actions precipitate a turning point in this story, a turning point in Norah's relationship with her brother and then with Aunt Florence. In this chapter, as elsewhere in the story, Kit Pearson captures in clear, identifiable terms Norah's utter misery and sense of being pulled in two directions.

The story of Norah and Gavin continues in two sequels, *Looking at the Moon* and *The Lights Go On Again*. Some things get easier for Norah, but growing up is growing up wherever you do it, and there's no easy way through that.

What Did Kit Pearson Read?

In addition to Ransome—Dick and Jane readers, Beatrix Potter, *Winnie-the-Pooh*, *The Moffats*, the legends of King Arthur, the Narnia books, *Little Women*, *The Princess and the Goblin*, Enid Blyton, *Emily of New Moon*. Kit devoured books—literally. Deep into a book she would absent-mindedly tear off a small corner of the page and eat it!

Beyond the Back Cover:
A Classroom Script

One of the really powerful things about reading a novel is that you come to own the characters. If the writer doesn't mention what color hair the main character has, then you are perfectly free to imagine—red, chestnut brown or black-and-white striped. Even when the writer does supply details, no two people will imagine those details in exactly the same way. "The pony-faced girl . . . " What image do you get? Big teeth? Kind eyes? Soft lips? Snub nose? Friendly but a bit skittish?

After you finish a book you have even more freedom. At that point, you the reader have as much right to figure out that character's future as the writer does. Starting with a pre-existing character, rather than starting from scratch, can be a good route into writing.

Start with a character from a book that you really like and know. It doesn't have to be the main character. Like Kit Pearson, you can pick a minor character from a favorite book. Now put on your gold hoop earrings and your shawl and gaze deep into your crystal ball. Do you see the future? Are the mists of time clearing away? If your fortune-telling skills need a little nudge, you might think about these questions:

What kind of work does your character do? Is it something that you could have predicted from her childhood interests and talents, or did she discover something totally new?

What is your character's name? Did Billy revert to the more dignified William? Did Squirt keep his nickname even when he became a heavyweight wrestler? Did Betsy change her name to Serena when she got to high school?

What does he look like? If he was the tallest boy in grade six, did he grow up to be a beanpole, or did he just stop growing in grade six? Did an ugly duckling grow up to be a swan, or did some swan end up as a regular duck?

What was her biggest problem when she was a kid? Does she still have that problem or has she solved it? How? Does she have another problem?

What is his temperament? Predictable or surprising? Did the class clown grow up to be the office wise-cracking practical joker? Did the motormouth grow up and join an order of silent monks? What happened?

Does your character get married? If so, to whom? To a character that you already know from the book or to someone totally different?

Take a couple of characters from your novel and have them meet at a high-school reunion twenty years later.

Write an obituary notice for one of your characters.

Harriet the Spy goes to college. Ramona the Pest stars in a senior citizens' punk rock group. James and the Giant Peach: Ten Years On. Harry Potter: The Untold Sequel.

You can send your character in any direction you like, as long as you can convince yourself that it is the same person. On the other hand, if you find your character turning into another person—go for it. It's your story now.

Keen readers in grades six and up can do this exercise choosing their own literary characters. For a group that is not so widely read, try this exercise using characters from a book that has been read aloud to the whole class. Compare the futures that they invent for the characters.

Revisits: Books That Grew From Other Books

Clarke, Pauline. *The Return of the Twelves.* When Charlotte Bronte (*Jane Eyre*) and Emily Bronte (*Wuthering Heights*) were children, they constructed an elaborate imaginary world along with their brother and sister. Part of their play was a box of wooden soldiers. After their deaths the soldiers disappeared. In this story, eight-year-old Max discovers them years later in an attic. He has inherited not just the soldiers but the whole living world of the Bronte imagination.

Eager, Edward. *Half Magic.* When Jane, Mark, Katharine and Martha read the stories of E. Nesbit, their own summer seems even more boring. Why can't they find something magic? Then a coin turns up that grants their wishes. Actually, it grants half of what they wish for. Therefore, they have to wish for twice as much as what they want. This gets complicated!

Greenwald, Sheila. *It All Began With Jane Eyre.* Why is Franny hiding in the hall closet with a bag of chips, a flashlight and a book? Reading Charlotte Bronte's *Jane Eyre* got her into trouble, so now she's trying teen problem novels. Worse trouble lies ahead. Read this hilarious novel about the hazards of really getting into what you read.

Horwood, William. *The Willows in Winter.* At the end of *The Wind in the Willows*, Kenneth Grahame tells us that wild Toad turned over a new leaf. Author William Horwood says, "I didn't believe it then and I don't believe it now." Remember the unsquelchable Mr. Toad in his car, menace of the roads? In this story he takes to the air. Rat, Mole and Badger are at their wits' end.

Mace, Elizabeth. *Out There.* The time is the future. There is no childhood. Four children are laboring in a quarry. They have no families, little food and no freedom. Their cruel boss beats them. But one of the children has a book—a tattered old book that tells of another time, when children were allowed to play. This book inspires the four to attempt an escape. The book is

Arthur Ransome's *Swallowdale*.

Major, Kevin. *Eating Between the Lines*. Getting lost in a book is one thing. But Jackson really gets into his reading. He ends up battling the Cyclops with Ulysses, being rescued by Huckleberry Finn and turning into Romeo—balcony, Juliet and all. Strange (and funny) goings-on for a motor-mouth teenage boy in love.

Piano Four Hands:
C.S. Lewis

Brothers. Jack and Warren. Jack says of Warren, "We were allies from the first." Warren says of Jack, "His friendship was the greatest happiness of my life."

Who are these boys? Let's spy on them for a few minutes.

We are in Ireland. It is damp. Raindrops trickle down the windows of a big house in the country. In the attic of this house is a room called the "dayroom." It is a sort of living room just for kids, no adults allowed. It is filled with hand-me-down furniture, toys and piles of books. The walls are decorated with pictures cut out of magazines. It is messy and comfortable.

In this room are two brothers. Ten-year-old Warren is sitting at a table chewing his pencil. He is working out a railway timetable for his imaginary land, a land called India. India started out being the real India but has recently been transformed, in Warren's stories, into an island.

Seven-year-old Jack is lying on the floor drawing. (Jack's real name is Clive but he hates it.) He is making a picture of a rabbit in medieval armor. The rabbit-knight is one of the inhabitants of Jack's invented world, a place called Animal-Land. Animal-Land is connected to Island-India by steamship service. Warren has worked out the details.

Jack is a chatterbox and he begins to talk, half to himself, about a forthcoming tournament at which his rabbit-
knight is to joust. Warren asks Jack's advice about a tricky
new branch line, and together they consult one of their
many maps of India/Animal-Land—maps that are painted
in every color of Jack's paintbox.

Warren is home from boarding school for the holidays.
Jack doesn't go to school. His mother teaches him.
Sometimes the boys visit relatives; they have parties with
other children. But really they just want to be left alone
with their stories, books, pictures, toys and each other.

The linked imaginary lands of India and Animal-Land
went on for years, until both boys were teenagers. A couple of years after the scene we have spied on, Warren and
Jack's mother died. Their father, in his grief, withdrew
from the boys. The brothers' shared sorrow brought them
even closer. And their imaginary worlds grew closer to
become one world that they named Boxen. Animal-Land
became Boxen in the past. India became Boxen in the present. Jack, who began to be fascinated with history and
mythology, set about writing a complete history of Boxen.
Together the brothers expanded and perfected their imaginary kingdom, making it more and more detailed and
real. Like playing a piano four hands, they created something together that neither could have done alone. And
they did it all for the pleasure of it.

As an adult, Warren took his talent for organization
into the army. Jack became a very popular and successful
university teacher, and he continued to write. He wrote
books on literature, history and religion. He wrote an
autobiography. He wrote science fiction and fantasy novels. And he wrote the series of books for which he is best
remembered, *The Lion, the Witch and the Wardrobe* and
the six other Chronicles of Narnia.

In *The Lion, the Witch and the Wardrobe*, C.S. Lewis (he still didn't like Clive so he just used his initials) tells the tale of four children who travel through the back of a cupboard to a fantasy land called Narnia. Narnia is a world of witches, giants, dwarves, castles, tree-fairies, royalty, magic spells, wickedness and heroism. It even has dressed animals, just like Boxen. But Boxen was a private world, never meant for outsiders, whereas the Narnia books were written to be published, to be shared by readers everywhere. And they have been. Narnia is one of the most famous imaginary lands in literature. It isn't surprising that C.S. Lewis was so good at creating imaginary lands. He had, after all, been practicing for it his whole life.

The Lion, the Witch and the Wardrobe: A Sneak Preview and Read-Aloud Suggestion

In one way Narnia does show its roots in Boxen. Like Boxen, Narnia contains both ordinary and fantastic worlds. C.S. Lewis is a master at making us feel right at home in a totally other-world setting. Even when life-and-death matters are at stake, C.S. Lewis never forgets that people have to eat, and he is one of the best food-describers of all time.

Midway through *The Lion, the Witch and the Wardrobe*, in Chapter 7, "A Day With the Beavers," the children get lost in a wintery wood. There is a feeling of quietness and danger. A friendly beaver appears and adds to the feeling of suspense with mysterious talk of "the arrest," "the enemy" and the awe-producing name of Aslan. We are in a place where even the trees are listening. There is also a hint of trouble to come when Lewis tells us that a horrible idea came into Edmund's head.

Into this tension comes a dinner invitation. The beaver invites the four children home to his warm, cozy lodge and he and his wife serve what sounds like the most delicious dinner one could imagine on a cold winter's night. Lewis's enthusiasm for buttered potatoes and marmalade roll is totally contagious. The children take a welcome break from their wanderings and so do we the readers. And we need it, because the next chapter involves an introduction to the politics of Narnia and the chilling answer to what Edmund's horrible idea was.

The Narnia books have wide appeal, even to children with no particular interest in fantasy. They are also very straightforward in style. Read them aloud to grades three to six.

What Did C.S. Lewis Read?

A Connecticut Yankee in King Arthur's Court (Mark Twain), *Five Children and It, The Phoenix and the Carpet, The Amulet* (E. Nesbit), *Gulliver's Travels* (Jonathan Swift), Beatrix Potter (his favorite was *Squirrel Nutkin*), H.G. Wells' science fiction, Norse mythology and anything in his parents' large library. In *Surprised by Joy* he remembers:

There were books in the study, books in the drawing room, books in the cloakroom, books (two deep) in the great bookcase on the landing, books in a bedroom, books piled as high as my shoulder in the cistern attic, books of all kinds . . . books readable and unreadable, books suitable for a child and books most emphatically not. Nothing was forbidden me.

Tandem Writing: A Classroom Script

Any of the writing ideas in this book can be adapted to sharing with a friend. The friend might be a brother or sister, a school friend, someone you know only in the summer, or someone you met on the Internet. You don't have to think alike or have the same interests. Jack and Warren certainly didn't. But you have to respect and enjoy each other. No put-downs.

Try some of these ideas:

◆ Combine two desert islands. Perhaps they merge, using the best ideas of each, or perhaps their inhabitants somehow visit each other, or otherwise set up communication.

◆ Raid the recycling box for newspapers and settle down with a friend. Read bits aloud to each other. Or get out your scissors and do this at a distance. Fax newspaper gems to your friend across the country.

◆ Get together with a friend and write a skit based on a fairy tale. Act it out. Videotape it. Or try illustrating or animating a favorite story. What about a musical?

◆ If you are lucky enough to have a friend that you really trust, try introducing your imaginary being to her imaginary being.

◆ Sometimes other people's family stories seem better than your own. And sometimes adults are more willing to tell these stories to someone who is not related. Adopt someone else's parents temporarily.

◆ Do you and a friend have similar feelings on something in the world? Write a joint letter to the editor.

◆ Set up a riddle exchange club, either in person or electronically.

◆ Tell your friend your dreams. Ask about his.

◆ Even a diary, which seems like the most private writing of all, can be shared. Louisa May Alcott's mother read her diary (with Louisa's permission!) and made comments in the margin, turning the diary into a kind of written conversation. And way back in the nineteenth century two French brothers wrote a joint diary that went on for twenty years, only ending when one brother died.

The great thing about these joint writing experiments is that you can't lose. You might end up producing something with your friend that pleases you both. On the other hand, you might end up with nothing except an afternoon or a week or a year of fun. Who cares? Not everybody needs to be a writer. But everybody needs to have a good time with friends. And it sure beats hanging out at the mall.

 Many of these ideas are a tandem adaptation of other exercises in this book and work best once some individual writing and thinking have taken place.

Tag-Teams: Books Written By Pairs

Ahlberg, Janet and Allan. *It Was a Dark and Stormy Night.* Antonio is a little boy who has been kidnapped by brigands. One dark and stormy night the bad guys ask for a story and Antonio begins, "It was a dark and stormy night . . ." Mr. and Mrs. Ahlberg invent a clever and funny story within a story within a . . .well, you get the idea.

Asimov, Janet and Isaac. *Norby and the Court Jester.* Mr. and Mrs. Asimov treat us to the story of a boy and his robot who go off for a holiday to the planet Izz, where they become embroiled in a plot involving the evil jester Ing.

Downie, Mary Alice and John. *Honor Bound.* The Avery family, loyal to the British king, are forced to leave their home in Philadelphia at the time of the American Revolution. They head north to Canada in this story of danger, suspense and survival, told by a wife-and-husband team.

Gal, Laszlo and Raffaella. *The Parrot.* Father and daughter Laszlo and Raffaella Gal join their writing (and painting) talents in this story of a beautiful maiden who is protected by a young prince-in-parrot disguise.

Howe, Deborah and James. *Bunnicula.* The goofy tale of a pet rabbit. He has fangs. He is nocturnal. And why are the vegetables in the fridge drained white and dry? Mr. and Mrs. Howe pretended that they wrote this story, but really we know it was written by Harold the dog.

Irwin, Hadley. *The Original Freddy Ackerman.* Colleagues Lee Hadley and Ann Irwin joined together to form the writer Hadley Irwin. In this novel Trevor spends the summer with two eccentric great-aunts and assumes a new identity. As "Freddie" he is dashing, brave, invincible, swift and incorruptible.

Keillor, Garrison and Jenny Lind Nilsson. *The Sandy Bottom Orchestra.* A summer in small-town U.S.A. for fourteen-year-old Rachel involves music and sports, embarrassing parents, a falling-out with a friend and many funny and engaging insights. A readable and warm-hearted novel from a husband-and-wife team.

Little, Jean and Maggie DeVries. *Once Upon a Golden Apple.* Aunt Jean and her niece Maggie join talents in this romp of fractured fairy tales.

Mazer, Norma Fox and Harry. *Heartbeat.* When someone saves your life, you are linked forever. This is the bond between Tod and Amos. When happens when they both fall for the same girl? Husband-and-wife writers explore the dilemma of the love triangle.

McKissick, Patricia C. and Frederick. *Sojourner Truth: Ain't I a Woman.* A husband-and-wife team collaborate on the biography of the freed slave who became a powerful activist for freedom and the rights of women.

A Picture and a Thousand Words: Virginia Hamilton

One day Virginia Hamilton was at an auction. She spied a big spool of green string, the old-fashioned kind that people once used to tie packages. Many people would have been unmoved by this string, but Virginia Hamilton has the soul of a collector, and collectors know good stuff when they see it. She took the string home, knowing it would come in handy, and when she got there she began idly weaving it between her fingers. After a while those woven creations became very individual and interesting shawls.

At the same time that Virginia Hamilton was auction-hopping and weaving, she was writing. In a book called *The Planet of Junior Brown*, Nightman, a young homeless boy in New York, finds a spindle of string and finger-weaves coats for himself and a friend. The image of these coats that appears in the last chapter of the novel is one of support and hope for the boys.

A few years later the motif of green weaving appears again, in a pair of images in M.C. *Higgins the Great*. The Higgins family lives on the side of a mountain deep in the country. Crossing one of the deep valleys is a suspension bridge cleverly woven from green vines. And, in one of the most arresting inventions in all children's books, there is an echoing image in the description of a huge rope-and-vine web constructed to link the houses that form the extended community of the Killburn family, M.C.'s neighbors. There is a joyousness about this construction and the gang of children who rest on it or bounce across it that contrasts with the many ominous images of this world.

The use of memorable and original images characterizes Virginia Hamilton's books. When she describes the starting points of her writing, she talks about chasing images that have disappeared around the corner of her mind and says, "I see stories in a series of pictures to which I add words."

A single image can be a rich starting point for a story, especially if it raises questions in the writer's mind. The image can be exotic, odd, beautiful, mysterious or as simple and ordinary as a piece of string.

Virginia Hamilton has a wide range of collecting interests. Have students visit her Web site (www.virginiahamilton.com), where they can see a selection from her frog collection. And, like all real collectors, she is always looking for additions to her collections. So, if your students have a frog joke, they might like to send it along.

Collections breed stories. Ask students who have collections to describe them and then to introduce the best thing in their collection to the group. (Prime collecting ages seem to be about grades four and five.)

For a stunning example of the use of collections in a story, see Lois Ehlert's picture book, *Market Day*. Ehlert creates collage illustrations using objects from her many collections. Guatemalan fabrics, ice-fishing decoys, African wood carvings and Indonesian carved mice all combine to make their own original story.

M.C. Higgins the Great: A Sneak Preview and Read-Aloud Suggestion

Virginia Hamilton's books are challenging to excerpt because her plots are very tightly woven and the meaning builds gradually over the course of the story. On the other hand, reading her work aloud is an excellent idea because a lot of the meaning lies in the rhythm of the words. It is also appropriate to experience her stories in a group context, because so many of her themes relate to the strength of community.

The plot of M.C. Higgins the Great includes the arrival of two strangers at M.C.'s mountain home. One is a scholar who makes recordings of folk music. The other is Lurhetta Outlaw, a strong, independent young woman whom teenaged M.C. is anxious to impress. In the second half of Chapter 8 and the first scene of Chapter 9, M.C. agrees to take Lurhetta with him on a swim through the "water tunnel" that connects a lake and a smaller pool. This is a foolish move, but M.C. is proud and stubborn and so is Lurhetta. The detailed description of their sixty seconds underwater shows how Virginia Hamilton gets inside the very bodies of her characters. This is a highly suspenseful scene and definitely not for the claustrophobic!

 Read Virginia Hamilton aloud to grades seven to nine.

Collecting Images: A Classroom Script

In her use of images as a starting point for writing, Virginia Hamilton joins the ranks of many other visually oriented writers. C.S. Lewis began *The Lion, the Witch and the Wardrobe* with an image of a faun standing in a snowy wood. Tim Wynne-Jones puzzled over an imaginary image of a grand piano being airlifted by a helicopter in the early stages of writing *The Maestro*. The Maina historical novels by Dominique Demers began with the single image of a young girl, dressed in leather, running across a headland.

A useful exercise for a writer involves a day of image-collecting. The equipment for this mission consists of a notebook and a pencil. The skills required are the ability to relax, notice and pay attention.

In this exercise the writer pretends to be a camera, with twenty-four exposures. Over the course of a day, which can include sleep so as not to miss something in a dream, the writer simply writes down, very briefly, descriptions of images. These pictures can be anything that catches attention, even just for a second. Gray lichen on a tree trunk, a piece of orange peel floating down the gutter, your own eyebrows, a house that looks like a face, a fly on the window, the pattern on the sole of a shoe, the shape of a paper clip.

The trick with this exercise is to be alert but not tense. This is not like big-game hunting where you pursue the image and nab it. It's more like bird-watching. You stay quiet and look very carefully. Once in the habit, you will be amazed by the infinite number of small things you notice and enjoy. Some of the images you collect may work themselves into stories, but even if they do not, a sense of amazement and delight at the immense variety of the world is a good place to start writing.

This idea is best suited to grades six and up. A shorter in-class version for younger children involves taking one mental photo of something in the classroom. In this case, extensive moving around should be encouraged. (What does the underside of the teacher's chair look like?) Expect a certain degree of chaos!

The Ordinary and the Fabulous: Selected Folktale Collections

Fairy-tale collections are a treasure trove of arresting images. Think about how we remember Rapunzel's long hair or the little pig's house of straw long after we've forgotten the details of the stories. Stories in a collection (as opposed to individual tales lavishly illustrated in picture books), give readers plenty of opportunities to recreate the images themselves. A story collection also gives the reader a longer, more leisurely visit to the particular fairy-tale world.

Clutesi, George. *Son of Raven, Son of Deer.* A collection of fables from the Tse-Shaht people. Fishermen raking shiny herring into their canoes; sharp-eyed Son of Eagle sitting on the top of a tall tree; the skinny legs of Boy Deer.

Cole, Joanna. *Best-Loved Folktales of the World.* A man who fishes up an island; a woman who appears from an orange; a tiny brownie with a long blue beard. This fat book has enough folktales to last a lifetime.

Crossley-Holland, Kevin. *British Folktales.* A boy the size of a thumb; a man with seaweed hair; a huge green cheese floating in a pond—fresh new versions of old stories.

Hamilton, Virginia. *Her Stories: African American Folktales, Fairy Tales, and True Tales.* Illus. Leo and Diane Dillon. An old woman who takes off her head to comb her hair; a glove that turns into a cat; a beautiful red fish wearing a golden crown—a story collection rich in images.

Jade and Iron: Latin American Tales from Two Cultures. Trans. Hugh Hazelton, ed. Patricia Aldana, illus. Luis Garay. Rainbow-colored horses; a drawing that comes to life; a giant worm—fourteen stories from a varied and sturdy tradition.

McCaughrean, Geraldine. *The Golden Hoard: Myths and Legends of the World.* A rainbow that transforms itself into a snake by drinking its own magic; an aged king sitting on his throne carving chess pieces. These lesser-known stories from everywhere are beautifully retold.

Minard, Rosemary. *Womenfolk and Fairy Tales.* A trapdoor that leads to a tunnel inside a mountain; twelve ravens speeding across the sky; a house with a thousand windows—plus a whole book full of smart girls.

Osborne, Mary Pope. *Mermaid Tales from Around the World.* Illus. Troy Howell. A white tent set on the shore filled with trinkets to lure thrice-lovely Nastasia from the sea. A dozen tales celebrate a wide variety of women of the water.

Wolkstein, Diane. *The Magic Orange Tree and Other Haitian Folk Tales.* A young woman who sinks into the earth as she weeps; a dancing owl; an egg filled with silver—memorable stories collected by a master storyteller.

Yashinsky, Dan. *Ghostwise: A Book of Midnight Stories.* A boogie-woman covered in dirt five inches thick; a face that cracks like an egg; a million mice sailing in a huge tree-boat—and a reminder that not all fairy tales are set in the once upon a time.

A Tale of Two Journals :
Louisa May Alcott and
L. M. Montgomery

A young girl is writing at her dining-room table. She is concentrating very hard. Let's look over her shoulder.

> *Mr. Parker Pillsbury came, and we talked about the poor slaves. I had a music lesson with Miss P. I hate her, she is so fussy. I ran in the wind and played be a horse, and had a lovely time in the woods with Anna and Lizzie. We were fairies, and made gowns and paper wings. I "flied" the highest of all. In the evening they all talked about travelling. I thought about father going to England, and said this piece of poetry I found in Byron's poems:—*
> *"When I left thy shores, O Naxos,*
> *Not a tear in sorrow fell;*
> *Not a sigh or faltered accent*
> *Told my bosom's struggling swell."*
> *It rained when I went to bed, and made pretty noise on the roof.*

A day in the life of a happy, energetic ten-year-old girl. A girl who loves to play and make believe and dress up. A reader and a writer.

This is Louisa May Alcott. At this point in her life she and her parents and sisters (Anna, twelve; Lizzie, eight;

and three-year-old Abby May) are living at a kind of experimental farm commune called Fruitlands, near Boston. The members of the commune call themselves the "Consociate Family." There are acres to play in and trees to climb. There are her sisters and neighbors up the road to play with. Children are treated with respect, asked their opinions, invited to join in discussions. On the other hand, the Consociate Family is very strict. No meat, cold baths, no use of farm animals, long discussions of serious issues. The food is very boring—apples, bread and potatoes, over and over again. And there are an awful lot of adults around, butting in, expecting you to be good. Adults like the dreadful Ann Page (Miss P.) and Mr. Lane, who seems to hate fun in any form.

Worst of all, Louisa's parents are arguing. She hears her mother crying at night. The problem is an ongoing one— poverty. There is no money for the mortgage on Fruitlands, or for food. The crops are not thriving and Louisa's mother wonders how they will make it through the coming winter.

The Alcott family, like any family, is a mixture. There is love and irritation, good times and disaster, support and anger, harmony and tension. And Louisa records it all in her diary.

Fifty years later, a fifteen-year-old young woman in Cavendish, Prince Edward Island, is writing in her journal.

Thursday, Feb. 27, 1890.
Last night we went to Minnie's. We found the house full of company—Mr. & Mrs. Wallace Toombs, Maud, Herbert and Hammond Toombs, Mr. Rogerson, the Rustico school-teacher, Miss Gordon, and Nina and Stanton Macneill. We had a glorious

time. We played all kinds of games and laughed
until the house echoed. After lunch we all went out
to the kitchen. Joe, the French boy, played a tune on
his jewsharp and we danced an eight-hand reel. It
was my first attempt at dancing and I danced with
Stanton Macneill. I stayed all night with Pensie
again. Oh, I've had such a good time this week! It
must be awfully nice to live in a house where there
are lots of people.

My mother died when I was a baby. I have
always lived with Grandpa and Grandma Macneill.
Father is away out west in Prince Albert,
Saskatchewan. He is married again. I have never
seen my stepmother or my two-and-a-half-year old
sister, Kate. I have always had a good home here but
sometimes it is very lonesome. Grandpa and
Grandma always seem so averse to my going any-
where or having my friends here.

This is another smart, imaginative, fun-loving teenager
who enjoys dancing, sleepovers and gossip, who has her
eye on a particular boy. She is a keen reader, a person who
tries very hard to be good and a person with sadness in
her life. This is Lucy Maud Montgomery, known as
Maud.

Maud's grandparents are loving but they are old and
stern and set in their ways. They want routines and quiet.
Maud craves company, lively talk, dancing, friendship,
drama, excitement, humor and poetry. These desires are
squelched by her grandparents. But they can't stop her
from feeling. And they can't stop her from writing. In her
diary Maud is free to be her real self.

By 1868, Louisa was thirty-five years old, a hard-
working professional writer. She had published stories

for magazines, articles for newpapers, plays, fairy tales for children and a novel for adults. She was the chief financial support for her parents and sisters, and money was still a problem. When a publisher friend asked her to write a "nice book for girls," Louisa was not enthusiastic: "Mr. N. wants a *girls story*, and I begin 'Little Women.' Marmee, Anna, and May all approve my plan. So I plod away, though I don't enjoy this sort of thing. Never liked girls or knew many, except my sisters, but our queer plays and experiences may prove interesting, though I doubt it."

Never was a writer more wrong. *Little Women* was a runaway success. It made Louisa May Alcott a famous woman, and a rich one.

In writing *Little Women*, Louisa May Alcott was really inventing a whole new kind of book—a story with realistic people—that concentrated on the small details of everyday life. She had no models for this kind of book. For material she simply used her own family. The Alcott family became the March family. Her mother became Marmee, older sister Anna became Meg, younger sister Elizabeth became Beth. And the baby of the family, May, had the letters of her name rearranged to become Amy. As for herself, she became Jo, the energetic, impetuous and passionate heroine of the novel, and everyone's favorite character.

Even after 130 years the March family still strikes readers as realistic and familiar. One reason for Louisa May Alcott's success was that she had had years of practice in describing everyday life. In her daily journal entries she had been storing away a rich treasure-house of material—the events, celebrations, frustrations, joys and tensions of a real family. She wrote *Little Women* in just eight months. But really Louisa May Alcott had been writing this book her whole life.

Like Louisa May Alcott, Maud Montgomery became a writer. By the time she was thirty years old, she had published articles, poems and many short stories in magazines like *Good Houskeeping, Boys' World* and *Family Story Paper*. Her father and grandfather were dead and Maud still lived with her increasingly grumpy and rigid grandmother.

One evening she was browsing through her notebook, an ideas book in which she kept bits of description, plot and character. She came across the following:

"Elderly couple apply to orphan asylum for a boy. By mistake, a girl is sent them."

With this bare bones plot snippet, Maud began to write, and what appeared on the page was a girl called Anne. Red-haired orphan Anne was high-spirited, imaginative and a non-stop talker. She told the truth with gusto and she got into a lot of trouble.

Over the next year or so Maud wrote, with great pleasure, *Anne of Green Gables*. Anne is now famous worldwide. The book and its sequels have been translated into many languages. Anne has been transformed into a play, a musical, a television series, a doll. Thousands of tourists visit Prince Edward Island every year to see Anne country. In Japan there is a whole theme park devoted to *Anne of Green Gables*. Anne is mega.

What's the magic formula? The secret is that Anne, like Jo before her, is real. L. M. Montgomery really remembered what it felt like to be eleven years old. And one of her important sources of memory was her journal.

We were picking potatoes all day up in our hill field. I don't think anybody ever got to such a pitch of virtue as to like potato-picking. I hate it! But since I

*had to I was glad it was up in the hill field because
I love that field.*

Is this Anne speaking? It sounds just like her. But, no,
it is fourteen-year-old Maud, recording her life in her
journal, learning to be a writer by writing.

For an introduction to Louisa May Alcott and her world see All
Alcott: The Louisa May Alcott Web at http://www.alcot-
tweb.com. The Anne of Green Gables Home page is at
http://yoyo.cc.monash.edu.au/ ~frosty/anne.html.

Little Women and *Anne of Green Gables*: A Sneak Preview and Read-Aloud Suggestions

Little Women and *Anne of Green Gables* are now old-
fashioned. Their heroines wear quaint clothes and don't
carry cell phones. The books seem to show us a simpler,
gentler world. But this fuzzy-edged portrait of an ideal-
ized past is not what made the books popular when they
were published and it is not what makes them good
reads today. What makes these books real is that both
Montgomery and Alcott wrote about genuine emotions.
For example, in remarkably similar scenes, both writers
wrote very convincingly about rage.

In Chapter 8 of *Little Women,* Jo gets fed up with her
pesky little sister Amy and refuses to take her to the theater. When Jo returns from the theater, she notices that her
notebook, in which she writes stories, is missing. After
some fierce questioning, she discovers that Amy has
thrown the book into the fire. Jo loses her temper completely, shakes Amy until "her teeth chattered in her
head," and vows never to forgive her as long as she lives.

The object of Anne's anger is a neighbor, Mrs. Lynde.

Their first meeting, in Chapter 9, "Mrs. Rachel Lynde Is Properly Horrified," doesn't go well. Mrs. Lynde looks Anne up and down and pronounces judgment on her red hair and freckles. Anne, consumed with rage, stands before the neighbor, stamps her foot and vows undying hatred and unforgiveness, "passionate indignation exhaling from her like an atmosphere."

When Louisa May and Maud were young, children were not encouraged to express their emotions. These scenes are so fierce that one suspects both writers remembered the angry feelings of their childhoods, their responses to neglect or disrespect, and allowed their fictional heroines to express emotion in real, convincing, familiar ways.

Writers of this era had a more leisurely style than we are used to. The first sentence of *Anne of Green Gables*, for example, is 149 words long, which no editor would tolerate these days! If we can slow down a bit, however, both *Anne of Green Gables* and *Little Women* make excellent read-alouds. Because they are long books they create a satisfying feeling of being totally immersed in another world. Try them with students in grade five and up.

What did Louisa May Alcott and L. M. Montgomery read?

Louisa May read *The Vicar of Wakefield* by Oliver Goldsmith, Harriet Beecher Stowe's *Uncle Tom's Cabin*, *Robinson Crusoe* and the novels of Walter Scott.

Maud read Hans Christian Andersen's *Fairy Tales*, *King Solomon's Mines* by H. Rider Haggard, "The Lady of the Lake" by Walter Scott, *The Last of the Mohicans* by James Fenimore Cooper.

They both read John Bunyan's *Pilgrim's Progress* and *The Pickwick Papers* by Charles Dickens.

Maud was as enthusiastic about her reading as she was

about everything else. She writes about reading "The Lady of the Lake":

I used to pore over it in the old schoolhouse when I should have been wrestling with fractions—or when the teacher thought I should. But, all the same, it did me more good than the fractions would ever have done. It was nourishment for the heart and mind and soul.

Diary Writing Ideas: A Classroom Script

Got up. Had Shreddies. Went to school. Did my paper route. Watched TV. Went to bed.

Your pencil grinds to a halt. Your fingers grow paralyzed on the keyboard. Many people have this experience when they begin keeping a diary. What's to say?

If you are a lapsed diary writer, or if the thought of keeping a diary makes your brain go numb, perhaps you have a limited idea of what a diary can be. One thing a diary can be is a chronicle of daily events. Some people enjoy capturing the ordinary facts of their lives—what they ate, the weather, what came in the mail, the bank balance. They simply like keeping records. It is a kind of collection.

If you are this kind of diarist, keep your diaries safe, because they will be fascinating to your great-grandchildren. This information—how ordinary people spend their days—is hard to find out about the past.

If you are not this sort of diary keeper, consider experimenting with other kinds of diaries.

A Trip Diary. Buy a nice notebook for your next holiday. Holidays are good for diary writing because there are lots of new things to see and experience. You also often have more time for writing when you're on holidays. And a trip diary makes a better souvenir than those pink plastic totem pole salt and pepper shakers.

Sorting Out Feelings. A diary makes a good friend when you are miserable. L.M. Montgomery once wrote that if it were not for her diary, into which she could spill her feelings, she would have become sick with worry and frustration. Sometimes writing about your problems helps you discover what you should do. More often it helps just to write it all down. Diaries are a safe place to get angry, to cry, to complain, to be afraid. They don't get hurt feelings and they don't tell secrets.

The Commonplace Book. Heard a good joke lately? Found an article on your favorite singer? Come across a song lyric that really hit you? Got a postcard of a painting that you'd like to save? A program from a play? Found a line in a book that you would like to remember? A collection of bits like this is called a commonplace book, a scrapbook of stuff you like. Start with a big notebook. Copy things into it. Cut and paste. Print things off the Net and stick them in. Add your own comments. This book will be uniquely your own and, as someone once said, "Creating a book is too good an idea just to be left to writers."

A Grab Bag of Diary Ideas. Weather, emotions, opinions, resolutions, ambitions, dreams, family stories, gossip, quotations, your own poems, lists, fantasies, jokes, names, interesting words and phrases, things you want to find out about.

A final liberating hint about diaries: You don't need to do it every day.

It is the nature and purpose of diaries to be private. These writing exercises, therefore, are better done as individual projects; it is important to maintain student privacy.

Dear Diary: Books Written as Journals

Blos, Joan. *A Gathering of Days.* The year is 1830. Catherine is thirteen years old, but she must keep house for her widowed father and younger sister, help with the running of the farm and deal with a new stepmother and a runaway slave. Her journal is our window on her world.

Cleary, Beverly. *Strider.* In his diary fourteen-year-old Leigh Botts tells the story of joint custody, of a dog, that is—a dog that Leigh shares with his friend Barry. A dog can be a big help when you are having a fight with your friend, when your dad loses his job, or when you say something really stupid to a girl you like.

Cushman, Karen. *Catherine, Called Birdy.* "There was a hanging in Riverford today. I am being punished for impudence yet again, so was not allowed to go. I am near fourteen and have never yet seen a hanging. My life is barren." Birdy's diary, written in 1290, reveals the frustrations of a lively girl who sees life passing her by.

Fitzhugh, Louise. *Harriet the Spy.* Harriet is in training to be a writer. She observes the world around her and records her observations in a Spy Notebook. But when her school friends find the notebook, Harriet gets into deep trouble.

Gantos, Jack. *Heads or Tails: Stories from the Sixth Grade.* Jack has a creative approach to what you can keep in your diary. He keeps baseball cards, his stamp collection, photos, fortunes from fortune cookies, squished bugs and—oh, yes—these very funny stories from his life.

Hest, Amy. *The Private Notebook of Katie Roberts, Age 11.* Katie's notebook is the friend to whom she tells her feelings about her new stepfather, her move from New York City to Texas, her need for a best friend and her big plan for getting her old life back.

Jones, Robin D. *The Beginning of Unbelief.* Hal begins this journal to get rid of somebody. The somebody is his childhood imaginary friend, Zach. As Hal pushes Zach deeper and deeper into the science-fiction universe he has created in his journal, the events of Hal's own life start to make sense.

Sterling, Shirley. *My Name Is Seepeetza*. Twelve-year-old Seepeetza is two people. At the Indian residential school she is Martha. At home on her family ranch she is Seepeetza. These two selves come together in her journal, where she reveals the miseries of school, the fun of summer holidays and the joyous escape of reading.

Townsend, Sue. *The Secret Diary of Adrian Mole Aged 13 3/4*. In his diary Adrian reveals himself as a deeply sensitive poet-in-the-making. The trouble is that nobody notices. Not his parents, not his friend Nigel, not Pandora of the beautiful hair, not even his dog. Only his diary knows the real Adrian Mole.

Real-Life Journals:

Filipovic, Zlata. *Zlata's Diary: A Child's Life in Sarajevo*. When Zlata begins her diary at age ten, life is ordinary. She writes of family, school, sports and the Madonna fan club. But then the bombs begin to fall on her home city of Sarajevo. Zlata lives through the pain and fear of life in a war zone and records her feelings in her diary.

Frank, Anne. *The Diary of a Young Girl*. This document of a young Jewish girl in hiding from the Nazis in World War II is probably the most famous diary of all time. That this book was rescued is a kind of miracle. Reading it makes history real and now.

Hunter, Latoya. *The Diary of Latoya Hunter: My First Year in Junior High*. This real-life diary, written over one school year, is a document of changes. In twelve-year-old Latoya's life in New York the events in her external world—travel, becoming an aunt, witnessing a crime—are mirrored in the growth she is experiencing in thought and spirit.

Parry, Caroline. *Eleanora's Diary*. The journal of a pioneer girl beginning in 1833, when Eleanora is ten years old. The voyage from England to the new world, a visit to a circus, funny comments about her family, descriptions of pets, silly poems and great little doodles make Eleanora's diary a delight to read.

On the Outside Looking In:
Katherine Paterson

"Did you see that new kid?"

It is recess. Pansy is holding court. Pansy is the queen of the grade seven girls. Her ladies-in-waiting glance toward the new kid, a short grade four girl standing by the door of the school. They nod.

"Look at her skirt."

Pansy's subjects obediently look.

"It used to be mine. My mother put it in the charity box when I outgrew it." Pansy gives a scornful giggle.

The ladies of the court giggle along.

"She talks funny," contributes Dorothy.

Pansy lowers her voice. She is about to divulge a state secret. "I'll bet she's a spy."

"A spy? What do you mean?"

"Well, she's a Jap, isn't she?"

Betty, the brave one, suggests otherwise. "I thought she was born in China, not Japan."

Queen Pansy squelches this rebellion with a look. "Either way, she's weird."

Meanwhile the new kid, aware of the glances and the giggles, has herself become a queen. Not the queen of a gang of girls, but the Queen of the United States, her new-old home. In her head she walks slowly up the aisle of a giant church. It is her coronation day. She is tall. She is as glamorous as a movie star. She is wearing a beautiful gown that was made especially for her and a crown with gold and jewels. She is going to be the best queen the United States ever had—wise, fair, not a show-off. She's never going to laugh at anybody or be unkind.

It is a good daydream. It helps. All the same, the schoolyard is a lonely place for the new kid.

This new kid is Katherine Womeldorf, nine years old, recent refugee from China, missionary kid, third child in her family, reader, inventor of stories. She was born in China to missionary parents. When she was five years old the war between the Chinese and the Japanese made it too dangerous for the family to stay in China so they returned to the United States. Katherine hated it. She longed to return to her real home. After a year the family did go back to China where they remained for a further two years until war again forced them back to America. This second return was very difficult for Katherine. She didn't fit in at school and the other children were suspicious of her because she came from China. During World War II there was distrust of Japan and Katherine's classmates didn't pay any attention to the difference between China and Japan. Katherine was a stranger, on the outside looking in.

Thirty-five years later Katherine, now Katherine Paterson, was a minister's wife, a mother of four children, and a writer. She had published three novels for children, all set in Japan. Two events in her busy life sowed the seeds of a fourth book. First she was diagnosed with a serious illness. Then her son's close friend died in an accident. In response to these events,

Katherine Paterson wrote *Bridge to Terabithia.*

Bridge to Terabithia is a story about friendship, especially friendship based on a shared creation of the imagination. It is a story about loss. And it is a story about not fitting in. The feeling of being excluded is one that Katherine Paterson explores in many of her books. When she was in grade one she didn't get any valentines on Valentine's Day. Her mother felt very sorry for her, and years later she asked Katherine why she had never written about that sad experience. Katherine replied, "But, Mother, all my stories are about the time I didn't get any valentines."

Katherine Paterson has written several shelves of books for children. She has won the Newbery Award twice and a bouquet of other prizes. She is one of America's most respected and best-known children's writers. So, has that timid fourth-grade outsider disappeared, vaporized by success and fame?

Not entirely. In *Gates of Excellence* she writes:

When I walk into a room full of well-dressed people, I never walk in alone. With me is a nine-year old who knows her clothes are out of a missionary barrel, her accent is foreign, and her mannerisms peculiar—a child who knows that if she is lucky she will be ignored and if unlucky she will be sneered at.

She goes on to say, however, that as an adult she knows something she didn't know as a kid. She knows that everybody feels this way sometimes. She looks at people and sees the timid nine-year-olds inside them.

This talent for seeing the whole person is a great gift for a writer, and for a friend. It is one of the great advantages of having once been a weird little kid on the outside looking in.

Bridge to Terabithia: A Sneak Preview and Read-Aloud Suggestion

Leslie Burke is the new kid in grade five at Lark Creek Elementary. Jesse Aarons, who has lived at Lark Creek his whole life, can't figure out this newcomer. She is obviously smart but she doesn't know important stuff. She doesn't know that you're supposed to dress up for the first day of school. She doesn't know that you're not supposed to bring yogurt for lunch. She doesn't know that girls don't play with boys at recess, that girls don't race boys, that girls aren't supposed to win.

In Chapter 3, "The Fastest Kid in the Fifth Grade," Leslie weathers her first day at the new school, and Jesse realizes that he wants this girl for a friend. But he also realizes that this friendship is going to be difficult. We get to know Leslie from the point of view of Jesse. Katherine Paterson, showing us the outsider from the outside, magically manages to let us inside this engaging and original character.

The illustration to this chapter shows us the school classroom seen through the window in the classroom door. It is almost an emblem of the outsider looking in.

It takes a lot of courage to make friends with an outsider. Jesse has this kind of courage. His friendship with Leslie causes him great happiness and then great pain.

 Bridge to Terabithia is the perfect grade five read-aloud. (Excellent for younger and older listeners, too, but especially good for grade five.) The only problem is that it is difficult to read it without crying. (On the other hand, why is that a problem? Why should we hide the fact that we are moved by literature?)

To read an interview with Katherine Paterson see The Official Katherine Paterson Web Site at http://www.terabithia.com/.

What Did Katherine Paterson Read?

Katherine Paterson read *The House at Pooh Corner*, *The Wind in the Willows*, *Peter Rabbit*, *Heidi*, *Little Women*, *Paddle to the Sea*. She calls them "flashlight books."

In *The Spying Heart* she particularly remembers three books that were very important to her when she was young.

When she was nine she read *The Secret Garden* by Frances Hodgson Burnett.

> *I think the reason so many of us have loved that book is precisely because we are homesick for a garden we have never visited. We long for a music we have never really heard.*

When she was eleven she read *The Yearling* by Marjorie Rawlings.

> *The wonderful harmony between child and beast is a reminder of Eden. But Flag dies; the harmony is destroyed. Jody must become a man and take on the responsibilities of a man. I wept over his loss, and I knew he had lost far more than a pet or even a companion.*

When she was sixteen she read *Cry, the Beloved Country* by Alan Paton.

> *It was this book more than any other that enabled me to discover myself. I was shattered by my discovery, but the very devastation made a kind of healing and growth possible. A great book can do this for a reader.*

Writing by Heart: A Classroom Script

The Victorian writer George Macdonald once wrote a story called *The Light Princess*. The much-longed-for baby princess in this story is cursed at her christening by a wicked aunt. The curse is that the child will have no sense of gravity. She is light, both in body (she floats upward if she is not weighted down) and in spirit (she is always cheerful and light-hearted). This does not seem like such a bad curse at the beginning. Who would not like to bounce around the ceiling or fly like a kite? Wouldn't it be great to be happy, happy, happy all the time? But as the Light Princess grows up, Macdonald demonstrates how she becomes a kind of monster. If you cannot feel sorrow, then you cannot ever really feel either compassion or joy. The Light Princess has to cry before she becomes a real human being.

Being human involves a wide range of emotions. That explains why stories, scenes and passages that contain a lot of emotion are frequently engaging and memorable.

The key to creating and recreating emotion in writing lies in the advice "Show, don't tell." Katherine Paterson is a brilliant model in this regard. For example, in Chapter 3 of *Bridge to Terabithia*, the character Jesse goes through a wide range of emotions—admiration, compassion, embarrassment, excitement, anger, satisfaction, disappointment, guilt and pleasure. But Paterson doesn't use these words. Instead we see Jesse running, turning red, doodling with his finger on his desk, nodding his head, slurping his milk and changing his seat on the school bus. We interpret what he is feeling from his actions.

In this chapter, as elsewhere, Katherine Paterson shows herself to be a careful observer. A large part of writing is simply paying attention. We all have two main sources of information and material to use. First of all we have ourselves. More than one writer has talked about the experience of being inside some strong emotion and then feeling one part of the brain slide away to look at the situation from the outside. "Ah-ha, so this is what it feels like to have made a total idiot of myself. Now, how could I describe this?" (In fact, a large number of writers recall this habit from a very young age, looking at themselves as though from the outside, and then describing the situation.)

Our other source of material lies in observing other people. We usually know when someone is angry or joyous or sorrowful even when they don't express it explicitly in words. Even very small children know this. What are the clues that we use to get this information?

Here are a few exercises to experiment with, to begin to establish the habit of close observation.

• Think of someone you know well, family member or close friend. Describe how she acts when angry. How does she move? What is her tone of voice? Does she use particular words or phrases when she is angry? What happens to her face?

• Take some time and observe a baby. Babies have rapid changes of emotion and they haven't learned to hide them yet. Describe what the baby does and then guess at what emotion is being expressed. Are there gestures that the baby makes that you recognize in yourself?

• Think about a situation that would have a lot of complicated emotion. For example:

1. A boy walking home from school sees a man abusing a dog. The boy wants to intervene but he is scared of the man so he does nothing.

2. A girl is accused of stealing a jacket from a locker at school. She is innocent. The principal has her come into his office and says, "It is all right. I know you are having

a difficult year at home. You can just tell me the truth and return the jacket and you won't be punished."

3. A girl has a job babysitting a toddler. She takes him to the playground. The toddler is playing in the sandbox when the girl meets a friend by chance. The two friends start talking and when the girl looks up, the toddler has disappeared.

Imagine what the character would be feeling in this situation. Then let us in on the character's emotions without using any "feeling" words. Restrict yourself to describing what the character says and does.

• Pick an emotion (anger, envy, jealousy, anxiety, fear, guilt, shame, relief, hope, sadness, depression, happiness, pride, love, gratitude, compassion) and remember an incident when you felt that emotion. Describe one specific thing that you did or said while in that situation.

 The "pick an emotion" exercise involves a relationship of trust between writer and reader. It is better attempted in an on-going writing situation, and is more successful at the end of the school year than at the beginning. Students are more likely to investigate and describe emotionally pitched situations from their own lives if they are reassured from the outset that their writing can remain private if they so choose.

These exercises are best suited to grades six and up.

Heart to Heart: Books to Make You Cry

Babbitt, Natalie. *Tuck Everlasting*. The Tuck family has a gift that has been longed for since the dawn of time, a gift that is really a curse. They offer it to young Winnie Foster, who then has to make a challenging decision.

Burnett, Frances Hodgson. *The Secret Garden*. This classic, a childhood favorite of many writers, is about healing. The healing of a neglected garden, the healing of a disabled boy, the spiritual healing of a neglected girl.

Doyle, Brian. *Up to Low*. Doyle can move the reader from laughter to tears in one short paragraph in this story of love, family, compassion and delicious onion sandwiches.

Fox, Paula. *The One-Eyed Cat*. When Ned took the gun without permission and fired it into the dark woods, his first worry was that he had been observed. But then the one-eyed cat appears and Ned feels a new chill at what he might have done.

Friesen, Gayle. *Janey's Girl*. When Claire spends the summer in the small town where her mother grew up, she makes some difficult discoveries about her mother, her father and herself.

Henkes, Kevin. *Words of Stone*. Blaze looks out his window one morning and sees a giant word picked out in stones on the mowed hill. So begins the friendship of Blaze and Joselle —a quirky, original summertime friendship that gives each of them a safe place to grow.

Howker, Janni. *Badger on the Barge*. In each of these five stories a young person encounters an old one. Helen kidnaps Miss Brady from the hospital. Sean discovers how complicated heroism is. And Liz hears the wonderful story of when ninety-one-year-old Sally Beck was a boy.

Johnston, Julie. *Adam and Eve and Pinch-Me*. Sara Moone, shifted from foster home to foster home, is absolutely determined to keep herself apart—from her new family, from her community, and from her own story. Then she encounters the Huddlestons.

Little, Jean. *Mama's Going to Buy You a Mockingbird*. Jeremy's father is dying, and his world will never be the same again. We travel with Jeremy on his painful emotional journey and rejoice in his strength and the love of his family.

Lowry, Lois. *The Giver*. Everything is wonderful in Jonas's community of nurturing, patient, loving families. No poverty, no hunger, no pain. Then he discovers what dark truth lies behind his safe, predictable world.

Mori, Kyoko. *Shizuko's Daughter*. Shizuko as a young woman was bold, artistic and independent. But she came to a place where she did not want to live. Yuki, her daughter, has the strengths of her mother—strengths she has to use to make sense of the tragedy in her life.

Paton Walsh, Jill. *Goldengrove*. A summer by the sea with a beloved grandmother and a favorite cousin. What could be better? The sea, the lighthouse, the sky—these things don't change. But this year there is a stranger in this world, and for Madge that changes everything.

Rylant, Cynthia. *Missing May*. May, who has been Summer's mother for six happy years, has died. Summer is lost. Hope and healing come in a very unexpected form.

Voigt, Cynthia. *Homecoming*. Four children, abandoned by their mother in a shopping center, take their future in their own hands in this story of a long and difficult journey to find a home.

Index

Abel's Island (Steig), 24
Abracadabra Kid, The
   (Fleischman), 112
Absolutely Normal Chaos
   (Creech), 60
Acquainted With the Night
   (Hotze), 107
Adam and Eve and Pinch-Me
   (Johnston), 167
Adams, Richard, 77
Ahlberg, Allan, 100, 138
Ahlberg, Janet, 100, 138
Alcott, Louisa May, 84, 93, 96,
   136-37, 146-47, 148-50, 152
Aldana, Patricia, 144
Alice's Adventures in Wonderland
   (Carroll), 69, 85, 88, 89, 110-
   15, 116-17
Alice's Adventures Underground
   (Carroll), 111
All-of-a-Kind Family (Taylor), 32
Amulet, The (Nesbit), 46, 135
Andersen, Hans Christian, 152
Anne of Green Gables
   (Montgomery), 26, 150-52
Arabian Nights, The, 16
Art of Flower Painting, The, 89
Asch, Frank, 100
Asimov, Isaac, 138
Asimov, Janet, 138

Babbitt, Natalie, 167
Baby (MacLachlan), 23
Baby Island (Brink), 23
Baby's Opera, The (Crane), 89
Back of Beyond (Ellis), 41
Badger on the Barge (Howker),
   167

Ballantyne, R. M., 16
Ballet Shoes (Streatfeild), 32
Bantock, Nick, 98
Barrie, J.M., 20
Beauty (McKinley), 41
Beginning of Unbelief, The
   (Jones), 156-57
Bell, William, 52
Ben's Dream (Van Allsburg), 86
Best-Loved Folktales of the
   World (Cole), 144
Birds Drawn From Nature, 89
Blos, Joan, 156
Blyton, Enid, 127
Bodger, Joan, 41
Boggart, The (Cooper), 66
Bomb, The (Taylor), 24
Bond, Nancy, 107
Bone From a Dry Sea, A
   (Dickinson), 107
Book of Nonsense (Lear), 89
Borrowers, The (Norton), 67
Bridge to Terabithia (Paterson),
   161, 162, 164
Bridges of Summer, The
   (Seabrooke), 24
Brink, Carol Ryrie, 23
British Folktales (Crossley-
   Holland), 144
Bronte, Charlotte, 130
Bronte, Emily, 130
Browne, Anthony, 85, 114
Buffie, Margaret, 107
Bunnicula (Howe), 138
Bunyan, John, 16, 152
Burnett, Frances Hodgson, 163,
   167

Canterbury Tales, The (Chaucer), 69
Carroll, Lewis, 69, 85, 93-94, 95, 108-11
Catherine, Called Birdy (Cushman), 156
Chaucer, Geoffrey, 69
Cheaper by the Dozen (Gilbreth), 31-32
Child's Garden of Verses, A (Stevenson), 26
Child's Play (Stevenson), 15
Clark, Joan, 107
Clarke, Pauline, 130
Clay Marble, The (Ho), 52
Cleary, Beverly, 100, 156
Clever-Lazy (Bodger), 41
Clutesi, George, 144
Cober, Alan, 85
Cole, Brock, 23
Cole, Joanna, 144
Connecticut Yankee in King Arthur's Court, A (Twain), 135
Cooper, James Fenimore, 152
Cooper, Susan, 66, 78-79
Coral Island, The (Ballantyne), 16, 20
Count of Monte Cristo, The (Dumas), 46
Coyote Columbus Story, A (King), 41
Crane, Walter, 89
Creech, Sharon, 60
Cresswell, Helen, 31
Crossley-Holland, Kevin, 144
Cry, the Beloved Country (Paton), 163
Curtis, Christopher Paul, 60
Cushman, Karen, 156

Daddy-Long-Legs (Webster), 101
Dali, Salvador, 114

Dark Is Rising, The (Cooper), 81
Daydreamer, The (McEwan), 36, 85
Dear Brother (Asch), 100
Dear Bruce Springsteen (Major), 100-01
Dear Mr. Henshaw (Cleary), 100
Deem, James, 77
Demers, Dominique, 143
DeVries, Maggie, 139
Diary of a Young Girl, The (Frank), 157
Diary of Latoya Hunter: My First Year in Junior High, The (Hunter), 157
Dick and Jane series, 127
Dickens, Charles, 79, 152
Dickinson, Emily, 26
Dickinson, Peter, 52, 85, 107
Dillon, Diane, 144
Dillon, Leo, 144
Disney, Walt, 19, 36
Doll, The (Taylor), 107
Downie, John, 138
Downie, Mary Alice, 138
Doyle, Brian, 31, 167
Dream Stealer, The (Maguire), 41
Dreamer, The (Rylant), 85-86
Dumas, Alexandre, 46
Durrell, Lawrence, 22

Eager, Edward, 130
Ear, the Eye and the Arm, The (Farmer), 66
Eating Between the Lines (Major), 131
Ehlert, Lois, 141
Eleanora's Diary (Parry), 157-58
Ella Enchanted (Levine), 41
Ellis, Sarah, 41
Emily of New Moon (Montgomery), 26, 127
Enright, Elizabeth, 31

Estes, Eleanor, 31
Eva (Dickinson), 52
Everybody's Favourites:
  Canadians Talk About Books
  That Changed Their Lives
  (Rae), 17
Exiles, The (McKay), 60

Fairy Tales (Andersen), 152
Falcon on the Baltic, The
  (Knight), 55
Falls, C.B., 19
False Face (Katz), 107
Family From One End Street, The
  (Garnett), 31
Farmer, Nancy, 66
Farthest Shore, The (LeGuin), 23
Filipovic, Zlata, 157
First Crossing of Greenland
  (Nansen), 55
Fitzhugh, Louise , 156
Five Children and It (Nesbit),
  135
Fleischman, Sid, 112, 122
Fly by Night (Jarrell), 85
Forbidden City (Bell), 52
Forbidden Fruit (Yee), 103
Forestwife, The (Tomlinson), 42
Fox, Paula, 167
Frank, Anne, 157
Friends of Kwan Ming, The (Yee),
  103
Friesen, Gayle, 167
Fry, Rosalie K., 23

Gal, Laszlo, 138
Gal, Raffaella, 138
Galax-Arena (Rubinstein), 77
Gambler's Eyes (Yee), 104
Gammage Cup, The (Kendall),
  66
Gantos, Jack, 156
Garay, Luis, 144
Garner, Alan, 60

Garnett, Eve, 31
Gates of Excellence (Paterson),
  161
Gathering of Days, A (Blos), 156
Ghostwise: A Book of Midnight
  Stories (Yashinsky), 145
Giant Cold (Dickinson), 85
Gilbreth, Frank, 31-32
Giver, The (Lowry), 168
Goats, The (Cole), 23
Golden Hoard, The: Myths and
  Legends of the World
  (McCaughrean), 144-45
Goldengrove (Paton Walsh), 168
Goldsmith, Oliver, 152
Good Zap, Little Grog (Wilson),
  77
Greenwald, Sheila, 130
Greenwitch (Cooper), 81
Grey King, The (Cooper), 81
Griffin and Sabine (Bantock), 98
Gulliver's Travels (Swift), 135

Haggard, H. Rider, 152
Half Magic (Eager), 130
Hamilton, Virginia, 140-41, 144
Hand of Robin Squires, The
  (Clark), 107
Handful of Time, A (Pearson),
  107
Hans Brinker (Dodge), 26
Harriet the Spy (Fitzhugh), 156
Harris and Me (Paulsen), 61
Hazelton, Hugh, 144
Heads or Tails: Stories from the
  Sixth Grade (Gantos), 156
Heartbeat (Mazer), 139
Heidi (Spyri), 163
Henkes, Kevin, 60, 167
Her Stories: African American
  Folktales, Fairy Tales and True
  Tales (Hamilton), 144
Hesse, Karen, 100
Hest, Amy, 156

Hide and Sneak (Kusugak), 63
His Banner Over Me (Little), 26, 27-28
Ho, Minfong, 52
Hob and the Goblins (Mayne), 66-67
Hoban, Russell, 122
Hobbit, The (Tolkien), 69, 70-71, 118
Hobby (Yolen), 42
Homecoming (Voigt), 168
Honor Bound (Downie), 138
Hope, Anthony, 46
Horwood, William, 130
Hotze, Sollace, 107
House at Pooh Corner, The (Milne), 163
Howe, Deborah, 138
Howe, James, 138
Howell, Troy, 145
Howker, Janni, 167
Huckleberry Finn (Twain), 131
Hughes, Monica, 43-44, 52
Hunter, Latoya, 157

Ingpen, Robert, 19
Into This Night We Are Rising (London), 85
Invitation to the Game (Hughes), 52
Irwin, Hadley, 138
Island, The (Paulsen), 24
Island of the Blue Dolphins (O'Dell), 23
Island of the Great Yellow Ox (Macken), 23
Islanders, The (Townsend), 24
It All Began With Jane Eyre (Greenwald), 130
It Was a Dark and Stormy Night (Ahlberg), 138

Jacob Have I Loved (Paterson), 23

Jade and Iron: Latin American Tales from Two Cultures, 144
Jane Eyre (Bronte), 26, 130
Janey's Girl (Friesen), 167
Jarrell, Randall, 85
Johnston, Julie , 167
Jolly Postman, The (Ahlberg), 100
Jones, Robin D., 156-57
Juster, Norton, 122

Karas, G. Brian, 85
Katz, Welwyn Wilton, 52, 107
Keeper of the Isis Light, The (Hughes), 44-45
Keillor, Garrison, 138-39
Kendall, Carol, 66
King Arthur, 127
King Solomon's Mines (Haggard), 152
King, Thomas, 41
Kipling, Rudyard, 79, 93
Knight, E.F., 55
Konigsburg, E.L., 60
Krykorka, Vladyana, 63
Kusugak, Michael, 62-64

Lady of the Lake, The (Scott), 152, 153
Lang, Andrew, 69
Last of the Mohicans, The (Cooper), 152
Lear, Edward, 89, 122
LeGuin, Ursula, 23
L'Engle, Madeleine, 122
Letters from a Slave Girl (Lyons), 100
Letters from Rifka (Hesse), 100
Letters from the Inside (Marsden), 101
Levine, Gail Carson, 41
Lewis, C.S., 83, 92, 132-34, 135, 142
Light Princess, The (Macdonald), 66, 164

Lights Go On Again, The (Pearson), 127
Lion, the Witch and the Wardrobe, The (Lewis), 133-35, 142
Little by Little (Little), 26
Little, Jean, 25-27, 139, 168
Little Lord Fauntleroy (Burnett), 26
Little Women (Alcott), 127, 149, 151, 163
London, Jonathan, 85
Looking at the Moon (Pearson), 127
Lord of the Rings, The (Tolkien), 70, 71
Lottridge, Celia, 39
Lowry, Lois, 168
Lyons, Mary E., 100

M.C. Higgins the Great (Hamilton), 140, 142
Macaulay, David, 106
Macbeth (Shakespeare), 16, 17
Macdonald, George, 66, 69, 164
Mace, Elizabeth, 130-31
Macken, Walter, 23
MacLachlan, Patricia, 23
Maestro, The (Wynne-Jones), 142-43
Magic Circle, The (Napoli), 42
Magic Orange Tree and Other Haitian Folk Tales, The (Wolkstein), 145
Maguire, Gregory, 41
Mahy, Margaret, 52, 122
Major, Kevin, 100-01, 131
Mama's Going to Buy You a Mockingbird (Little), 168
Marineau, Michèle, 52
Market Day (Ehlert), 141
Marsden, John, 101
Mary Poppins (Travers), 34, 35-36

Mayne, William, 66-67
Mazer, Harry, 139
Mazer, Norma Fox, 139
McCaughrean, Geraldine, 144-45
McEwan, Ian, 36, 85
McGraw, Eloise, 67
McKay, Hilary, 60
McKinley, Robin, 41
McKissick, Frederick, 139
McKissick, Patricia C., 139
Meddaugh, Susan, 77
Melville, Herman, 55
Mennyms, The (Waugh), 67
Merlin (Yolen), 42
Mermaid Tales from Around the World (Osborne), 145
Milne, A.A., 79
Minard, Rosemary, 145
Missing May (Rylant), 168
Moby Dick (Melville), 55
Moffats, The (Estes), 31, 124, 127
Monkman, William Kent, 41
Montgomery, L.M., 83, 95-96, 147-48, 150-51
Moorchild, The (McGraw), 67
Mori, Kyoko, 168
Moser, Barry, 85-86, 114
Motel of the Mysteries (Macaulay), 106
Mouse and His Child, The (Hoban), 122
Munsch, Robert, 63
My Name Is Seepeetza (Sterling), 157

Nansen, Fridtjof, 55
Napoli, Donna Jo, 42
Narnia series (Lewis), 127, 133
Nesbit, E., 32, 46, 79, 84, 130, 135
Nilsson, Jenny Lind, 138-39
Nonsense Omnibus, A (Lear), 122

Nonstop Nonsense (Mahy), 122
Norby and the Court Jester
   (Asimov), 138
Norton, Mary, 67

O'Dell, Scott, 23
Old Woman and Her Pig and Ten
   Other Stories, The (Rockwell),
   39
Once Upon a Golden Apple
   (Little), 139
One-Eyed Cat, The (Fox), 167
Ordinary Jack (Cresswell), 31
Original Freddy Ackerman, The
   (Irwin), 138
Osborne, Mary Pope, 145
Other Side of Silence, The
   (Mahy), 52
Out There (Mace), 130-31
Over Sea, Under Stone (Cooper),
   81
Owl Service, The (Garner), 60

Paddle to the Sea (Holling), 163
Parrot, The (Gal), 138
Parry, Caroline, 157-58
Passager (Yolen), 42
Paterson, Katherine, 23, 60-61,
   159-61, 163
Paton, Alan, 163
Paton Walsh, Jill, 168
Paulsen, Gary, 24, 61
Pearce, Philippa, 61
Pearson, Kit, 107, 124-26, 127
Peter Pan (Barrie), 20
Phantom Tollbooth, The (Juster),
   122
Phoenix and the Carpet, The
   (Nesbit), 135
Pickwick Papers, The (Dickens),
   152
Pie and the Patty-Pan, The
   (Potter), 91
Pilgrim's Progress, The (Bunyan),

16, 152
Planet of Junior Brown, The
   (Hamilton), 140
Poems and Songs of Middle Earth
   (Tolkien), 69
Potter, Beatrix, 87-89, 92-93, 94,
   127, 135
Preacher's Boy (Paterson), 60-61
Princess and Curdie, The
   (Macdonald), 66, 69
Princess and the Goblin, The
   (Macdonald), 69, 127
Prisoner of Zenda, The (Hope),
   46
Private Notebook of Katie
   Roberts, Age 11, The (Hest),
   156
Promise Is a Promise, A
   (Munsch), 63

Quincy Rumpel (Waterton), 32

Rackham, Arthur, 114
Rae, Arlene Perly, 17
Ransome, Arthur, 53-55, 79, 94,
   95, 130-31
Rawlings, Marjorie, 163
Rebecca of Sunnybrook Farm
   (Wiggin), 26
Red Fairy Book, The (Lang), 69
Return of the Twelves, The
   (Clarke), 130
Revenge of the Iron Chink, The
   (Yee), 103
Rider Chan (Yee), 103
Road to Chlifa, The (Marineau),
   52
Robinson Crusoe (Defoe), 16,
   55, 152
Rockwell, Anne F., 139
Rodgers, Mary, 61
Rootabaga Stories (Sandburg),
   122-23
Rubinstein, Gillian, 77

Rylant, Cynthia, 85-86, 168

Sailing Alone Around the World (Slocum), 55
Sandburg, Carl, 122-23
Sandy Bottom Orchestra, The (Keillor), 138-39
Saturdays, The (Enright), 31
Scott, Walter, 152
Sea Monkey Summer (Ware), 101
Seabrooke, Brenda, 24
Secret Diary of Adrian Mole Aged 13 3/4, The (Townsend), 157
Secret Garden, The (Burnett), 26, 163, 167
Secret of Roan Inish, The (Fry), 23
Sendak, Maurice, 85
Shakespeare, William, 16
Shizuko's Daughter (Mori), 168
Silver on the Tree (Cooper), 78, 79-81
Sir Gawain and the Green Knight, 69
Skurzynski, Gloria, 42
Sky Is Falling, The (Pearson), 126-27
Slocum, Joshua, 55
Sojourner Truth: Ain't I a Woman (McKissick), 139
Some of the Kinder Planets (Wynne-Jones), 123
Son of Raven, Son of Deer (Clutesi), 144
Spirits of the Railway (Yee), 104
Spying Heart, The (Paterson), 163
Stars Come Out Within, The (Little), 26
Steadman, Ralph, 19
Steig, William, 24
Sterling, Shirley, 157

Stevenson, Robert Louis, 14-17, 46, 83
Story of the Treasure Seekers, The (Nesbit), 32
Stowe, Harriet Beecher, 152
Streatfeild, Noel, 32
Strider (Cleary), 156
String in the Harp, A (Bond), 107
Stringbean's Trip to the Shining Sea (Williams), 101
Summer Switch (Rodgers), 61
Sun and Spoon (Henkes), 60
Surprised by Joy (Lewis), 135
Swallowdale (Ransome), 130-31
Swallows and Amazons (Ransome), 55, 56-57, 124-26
Sweetest Fig, The (Van Allsburg), 86
Swift, Jonathan, 135

T-Backs, T-Shirts, COAT, and Suit (Konigsburg), 60
Tailor of Gloucester, The (Potter), 90
Tale of Mr. Tod, The (Potter), 91
Tale of Mrs. Tiggy-Winkle, The (Potter), 91
Tale of Peter Rabbit, The (Potter), 87-88, 91, 163
Tale of Pigling Bland, The (Potter), 91
Tale of Samuel Whiskers, The (Potter), 91
Tale of Squirrel Nutkin, The (Potter), 90, 135
Tale of Tom Kitten, The (Potter), 91
Tale of Two Bad Mice, The (Potter), 91
Tales From Gold Mountain (Yee), 103
Taste of Salt (Temple), 52
Taylor, Cora, 107

Taylor, Sydney, 32
Taylor, Theodore, 24
Tehanu (LeGuin), 23
Temple, Frances, 52
Ten Small Tales (Lottridge), 39
3 NBs of Julian Drew (Deem), 77
Through the Looking Glass (Carroll), 115
Thurber, James, 123
Tolkien, J.R.R., 68-70, 84, 97-98
Tombs of Atuan, The (Leguin), 23
Tomlinson, Theresa, 42
Tom's Midnight Garden (Pearce), 61
Townsend, John Rowe, 24
Townsend, Sue, 157
Travers, P.L., 33-34
Treasure Island (Stevenson), 16, 17-19, 46, 55
Tuck Everlasting (Babbitt), 167
Twain, Mark, 135
Twenty Thousand Leagues Under the Sea (Verne), 46

Uncle Tom's Cabin (Stowe), 152
Up to Low (Doyle), 31, 167

Vagin, Vladimir, 100
Van Allsburg, Chris, 86
Verne, Jules, 46
Vicar of Wakefield, The (Goldsmith), 152
Voigt, Cynthia, 168

Ware, Cheryl, 101
Watership Down (Adams), 77
Waterton, Betty, 32
Watsons Go to Birmingham - 1963, The (Curtis), 60
Waugh, Sylvia, 67
Webster, Jean, 101
Wells, H.G., 79, 135

Whalesinger (Katz), 52
What Happened in Hamelin (Skurzynski), 42
Whipping Boy, The (Fleishman), 122
Who Is Frances Rain (Buffie), 107
Williams, Jennifer, 101
Williams, Vera, 101
Willows in Winter, The (Horwood), 130
Willy the Dreamer (Browne), 85
Wilson, Sarah, 77
Wind in the Willows, The (Grahame), 88, 130, 163
Winnie the Pooh (Milne), 79, 127
Wizard of Earthsea, A (LeGuin), 23
Wolf and the Seven Little Kids, The, 37
Wolkstein, Diane, 145
Womenfolk and Fairy Tales (Minard), 145
Wonderful O, The (Thurber), 123
Words of Stone (Henkes), 167
Wrinkle in Time, A (L'Engle), 122
Wuthering Heights (Bronte), 130
Wyeth, N.C., 19
Wynne-Jones, Tim, 123, 142-43

Yashinsky, Dan, 145
Yearling, The (Rawlings), 163
Yee, Paul, 102-03
Yolen, Jane, 42

Zlata's Diary: A Child's Life in Sarajevo (Filipovic), 157